"This delightful book tells everything you ever wanted to know but are afraid to ask about branding slogans and logos for your ears rather than your eyes. Fun reading about how to create a memorable impression of your product or company using words and sounds. It's a recipe for creating your company's virtual spokesperson who is heard but not seen."

James A. Larson, Chair
W3C Voice Browser Working Group
Manager, Advanced Human I/O
Intel Corporation

"Marcus has hit a home run. Not only is *Voice Branding in America* a detailed and well-researched exposition on the evolution of voice as a channel for corporate narrative, it is also a fun read! Marcus applies his considerable experience to telling the voice branding story firsthand, in a personal—and personable—style. Read it!"

Bruce Ballentine, EVP and Chief Scientist
EIG Labs

"Call your company's automated phone system right now. Listen to the recorded voice, and ask yourself: "If this were a real person, would I hire them to work as a customer service representative in my call center? Would this person give customers a good impression of our company's brand?" If the answer is 'no,' then quick—pick up the phone and call Marcus Graham at GM Voices!"

Lizanne Kaiser, Ph.D.
Senior Principal Consultant
Genesys Telecommunications Laboratories, Inc.

"Call centers are increasingly using interactive speech systems to make the most of every customer contact while controlling costs. Voice branding is a key part of this trend, and Graham's book is a pioneering work in helping companies understand the opportunity."

Bill Meisel, Publisher
Telephone Strategy News and Speech Recognition Update

S0-BZY-378

VOICE BRANDING IN AMERICA

by G. Marcus Graham

VOICE BRANDING IN AMERICA

Editor: Kay duPont
Copyright ©2004

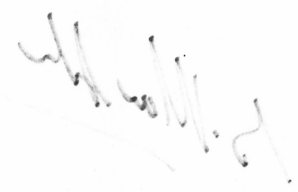

For more information, contact:
Vivid Voices, Inc.
2905 Jordan Court, Suite B-101
Alpharetta, GA 30004
www.vividvoices.com

Library of Congress Catalog Number 2004110382

ISBN: 0-9759895-0-2

10 9 8 7 6 5 4 3 2 1

DEDICATION

To the writer Ora Lindsay Graham, who convinced me
long ago that I can truly do and accomplish
anything my heart desires if I set my mind to it.

Thanks, Mom

TABLE OF CONTENTS

FOREWORD

I, too, have vivid memories from my childhood, dialing for the time and the temperature over and over again. I can hear those voices to this day, as well as remember the company sponsors. The power of voice branding is enormous and no one has more insight into the potency of voice branding than Marcus Graham. For two decades, Graham, and now GM Voices, has been an industry leader in the voice-branding arena and made enormous top- and bottom-line impact on a who's who list of clients.

As a devotee of branding and an advocate of building a "be the brand" culture that melds brand strategy with organizational structure and systems, I believe that Graham captures the essence of voice branding challenges facing many organizations today. This great book provides pragmatic, insightful, application-oriented takeaways that reflect the author's understanding of the evolving needs of the market and how to efficiently and effectively leverage ever-changing technology.

The author's insights on talent, brand identity and persona, technology systems and storytelling weave a powerful set of lessons for any businessperson interested in growing revenues and profits. What's so very exciting is that the book is written by an industry pioneer who, day in and day out, melds an understanding of branding theory and voice applications that keep GM Voices' clients coming back for more.

Timothy S. Mescon, Ph.D.
Dean and Dinos Eminent Scholar
Coles College of Business
Kennesaw State University

PREFACE

I remember hearing prerecorded voices on the telephone long before it occurred to me to do anything about it. In fact, I was just a kid when we used to call the Time and Temperature Lady over and over again just to hear the "correct time." I think it was a stepping stone to making prank calls to the local store. It went something like this: "Do you have Prince Albert in the can?" When the reply was Yes, my sisters and I would giggle and squeal, "You better let him out before he suffocates!" Then we'd hang up, laugh for a minute, and then call another store.

There were several variations of our Fun-with-the-Phone game: "I'm calling from the EMC Power Company. We're doing research on power usage in your area. Can you tell me, please, is your refrigerator running?" The most important part of this one was trying to sound like an adult. The best way to do that when you're 10 or 11 is to stand up, tuck your chin in, and talk from your throat. If we did a good job on the intro and they thought it was a legitimate call, we might hear, "Why, yes, it's running OK." Then the chorus of kids screamed, "Well, you better go catch it."

While this was clearly a popular past time for kids many years ago, it's gone by the wayside—relegated to the past by technology. Caller ID has taken the anonymity and the fun out of prank calls. Fortunately, you can still listen on the extension when your big sister is talking to her boyfriend on the phone, but as I recall, that didn't provide much in the way of interesting dialogue. It was mainly the sound of nervous breathing punctuated occasionally by a comment like, "What are you doing?" or "Do you really like me?"

Do you remember party lines? My grandmother was on a party line in the mid-1960s. In those days, the telephone's options were similar to the Model T's: You could have it in any color, as long as it was black. But they were cutting-edge communication devices in their day.

What will the "I remember when" story be for today's kids? It's always hard to imagine what it will be like in the future. "Way back in 2004, we had wireline phones, wireless phones, PDAs, desktop computers, laptops, smart wireless phones and GPS navigation. They were all just beginning to speak the same language of 1's and 0's. Maybe Dick Tracy's watch phone wasn't yet in mass production, but it was clearly here."

Remember when you actually dialed the phone? We used to play a game where we'd click on the receiver button (a little plastic dealie in the middle of each side of the cradle that held the handset). When the phone was placed in the cradle, the button was pushed down, which shut the phone off. We'd click it up and down quickly to simulate the clicks on the rotary dial as it returned to its resting position. We'd boast to our friends that we could dial a number without touching the dial. We'd place our bets, then dial the number in a Morse code fashion—clicking the button down once for each number.

I can still remember the number we had as kids in north Alabama: 773-6797. We didn't think about area codes because only sophisticated adults made long distance calls. It was very important when we got a long distance call. "Mr. Jones is on the phone. It's long distance!" It's hard to believe that it doesn't really make any difference today. Many industry pundits say that long distance is now a free part of some bundled packages.

As I said earlier, "Let's call the Time Lady" was a popular refrain in our house when things got dull. And, by today's definition, our house was really dull most of the time. There were only three VHF and one UHF television stations, and three or four radio stations. There was no cable, no Internet. Remote controls were a luxury that only rich people enjoyed. In fact, my dad used to call me his remote control: "Marcus, change it to Channel 11," he would say.

The Time Lady was neat. You could call her any time of the day and she was always relatively happy. We imagined this lady never went anywhere and continuously hung out by the phone. On the rare occasion we stayed up late, we'd sneak in a call to see if we could catch her sleeping, or at least groggy from not enough sleep.

It was exciting for me years later to meet the original Time and Temperature Lady while she was attending a communications show in Atlanta. Jane Barbe was a voice talent who lived in Atlanta and worked for Audichron, one of the companies that manufactured Time and Temperature systems. She was also the voice for Octel, one of the voice mail market leaders in the 80s and 90s before it was acquired by Lucent Technologies.

You might hear Jane say:
- *Good evening. At the tone, the time will be 8:15 and 32 seconds PM.*

- *The number you have reached, 862-4594, is being checked for trouble.*
- *Please try your call again later.*
- *We're sorry, you have reached a number that has been disconnected or is no longer in service.*

In 2002, Jane came to the GM Voices studios north of Atlanta to record a National Public Radio (NPR) segment about her adventures as the Time, Temperature and Voice Mail Lady. You can listen to the show via streaming media. Go to www.npr.org and search for "Jane Barbe." We're sorry to say that she passed away in 2003, but she's still heard millions of times a day.

When I started GM Voices, Inc., in 1985, I didn't have any grand plan for building a company. I was simply doing what I enjoyed—writing and producing audio in a recording studio. I was a voice talent "wannabe," but I was unable to pass the audition at advertising agency "cattle calls." I never got a paying voiceover job from an audition. I'm still not sure if I should be ashamed or proud of that. I still have my first voiceover demo from 1983, and it's really bad.

How bad is it? Let me put it this way: If I submitted my demo to our production manager, Robert Feldman, under an assumed name in an attempt to get voiceover work, he'd put it in a stack with the dozen or so he gets every week. When he had time to preview the demos, he'd probably listen to mine for about 10 seconds. That's how long it takes on a slow day to realize you don't need to listen any longer. It would end up in a box in a seldom-visited corner of the production storage room. With today's MP3 technology, it might even end up in the electronic equivalent of the box in the corner.

There is a remote possibility that if I happened by his office at the precise moment he was throwing away stuff he no longer needs, he might say something like, "Hey, Marcus (slight chuckle), you gotta hear this. It's priceless." Needless to say, I would not pass today's auditions either.

As a reasonably observant person, however, I did notice that the recordings on phone systems were almost always done poorly. So I contacted a few companies with the promise that I could make the after-hours or delay message on their phone system sound better. Luckily, the guys running the telecommunications departments at regular companies didn't have the same frame of reference about voice talent quality as the advertising guys.

I'd call in and record their current message, which they probably had never heard. I'd record my version in my friend's recording studio. Then I'd play before and after samples and they'd say, "OK, let's do it. How much?" I'd stammer a moment and say, "How about $200?" "OK." I was off and running.

The first few years, I was the main voice talent at GM Voices, but I realized early on that customers needed more choices. So I invited some of my voice talent friends to record samples and demos. I was soon presenting numerous voice actors to my clients so they could choose the voice talent with the right sound for their company. It was the beginning of voice branding in America.

Marcus Graham, CEO
GM Voices, Inc.
Alpharetta, Georgia

ACKNOWLEDGMENTS

Special thanks to the entire GM Voices staff who played a huge part in helping me put this book together. Particular appreciation goes to Vice President of Business Development Darrell Hensley, Production Manager Robert Feldman, Finance Manager Amy Neal, and Marketing Coordinator Valerie Hayden.

Others who provided insight and guidance include Mark Daley of Siemens; Lizanne Kaiser of Genesys; my editor Kay DuPont; cover designer Steven Parke; and Tony Messano.

Thanks to my children Rachel, Kelsey and Hunter, and my wife Karen.

INTRODUCTION

What is a voice brand and why am I writing about it? When I started GM Voices in 1985, my objective was to improve the sound quality of the prerecorded messages I heard on many phone systems. Almost all the delay and after-hours announcements at even very large and important companies were really bad. I'm talking embarrassingly bad. When I played before (what they had) and after (what I'd produced in a studio) samples for executives, they were shocked that such horrible messages were being delivered to their customers every day.

Today, many of those simple after-hours and on-hold messages have been replaced with powerful interactive voice response (IVR) computer telephony and speech recognition enabled systems that save companies millions every year. They're also helping organizations form a stronger bound with their customers by providing 24/7 access to information and the ability to transact business at their convenience.

Millions of Prerecorded Messages

In America, millions of phone systems play millions of prerecorded messages to millions of customers during millions of calls every single day! The impact of these messages on the companies and the people who call them is tremendous. The concern is not so much about sounding "pretty" when a customer calls. It's about building your brand and driving more profits to the bottom line. Voice branding.

Many of the automated voice systems in use today are good from a technical standpoint. When I say "automated," I'm referring to any system that uses prerecorded voice prompts or messages to guide the user in obtaining information, completing a task or routing a call. That includes anything on this list:

- Automated Attendant
- Voice Mail
- Interactive Voice Response (IVR)
- Automatic Call Distributors (ACD)

- Call Sequencers
- GPS Navigation Systems
- Automotive Voice Controls
- Automated Teller Machines (ATM)
- Kiosks
- Public Area Announcements
- Websites

Note that websites, kiosks, ATMs and other technologies are beginning to sprout voices. The branding guidelines in this book apply to any devices that use prerecorded voices.

Defining Voice and Brand

"Voice" means much more than the voice talent or voice actor people hear when calling you. "Voice" refers to the entire message of your company. The voice, words, call flow, personality, music and effects people hear on the automated systems are your company's "voice" to the world.

"Brand" is that intangible mixture of company, product and/or service attributes that embody your entire relationship with your customers. Your "Brand" is built one customer contact at a time through a wide range of channels. Over time, these accumulated "TouchPoints" become the brand in the mind of your customer.

This book focuses on the broad issues of branding as they relate to prerecorded voices and on how to implement an enterprise-wide Voice Branding Initiative (VBI). Corporate America's acceptance of speech recognition technology has dramatically raised the level of naturalness and quality expected in prerecorded voice applications. For a broader and more technical understanding of Voice User Interface (VUI) and speech recognition solutions, I'd recommend the following books:

- *The Art and Business of Speech Recognition: Creating the Noble Voice* by Blade Kotelly
- *Voice User Interface Design* by Michael Cohen, James Giangola and Jennifer Balogh
- *How to Build a Speech Recognition Application* by Bruce Balentine and David P. Morgan

Top 100 Voice Brands

It's noted a number of times in this book that voice branding is a new concept.

I'll explain why it's new and provide a little history from my 20+year industry perspective. Over the years, I've been asking leaders in marketing, branding, telecommunications and speech recognition this question: **"What's the status of voice branding in America?"**

The time is right to formalize the process of reviewing and ranking the best voice brands in business. That's why we created the Top 100 Voice Brands ranking that will debut Fall 2004. We're seeking nominations for good, bad and ugly voice brands in the marketplace today. We'll call them, record them, and put them on the Web for everyone to hear. A panel of industry experts will review them and select the Top 100 Voice Brands in America.

Our objective in creating this independent ranking is to establish a venue where we can quantify the quality of voice brands. Visit the Website to hear voice brands already nominated, to make additional entries you feel should be considered, and to learn more about the Top 100 Voice Brands. www.top100voicebrands.com

PART I: BRANDS AND BRANDING

What Is a Brand?

So what is a brand? And when you're "branding," what exactly are you doing? The best way to define the term "brand" is by first thinking about some of the products and services you buy every day. What comes to your mind when you think of the following categories?

• Hotels	• Soft drinks
• Fast food	• Ketchup
• Computers	• Gasoline
• Tools	• Golf balls
• Toothpaste	• Door locks

Chances are that you came up with many company and product names without great effort. They were neatly tucked away in your mind after years, or even decades, of reminders from their marketing departments and the media.

Successful brands are those products, services or combinations that occupy a special place in the consumer's mind where they are the only viable choices. In our discussion, I'll refer to them as "solutions."

A brand elevates purchases based on need to the realm of desire. By emotional, I mean how a brand engages consumers on the level of the senses and emotions, how a brand comes to life for people and forges a deeper, lasting connection.

— Marc Gobé
Emotional Branding

The power of a brand lies in its ability to influence purchasing behavior. But a brand name on a package is not the same thing as a brand name in the mind.

— Al and Laura Ries
The 22 Immutable Laws of Branding

Your brand is critical—as the container for all of your customer interactions with your company, it's the heart and soul of your company.
>—Sergio Zyman
>The Zyman Group

A brand is a promise of a relationship and a guarantee of quality. It establishes a relationship between a company and its audiences. A strong brand can and will differentiate, create a preference, command a premium.
>— Alycia Perry
>*Before the Brand*

What is Branding?

Branding is the act or process of building the brand's value in the mind of the consumer. Building a connection with the consumer that drives them to reach past the competing solution for yours is what branding is all about. But how are those bonds with the customer created?

One TouchPoint at a Time

TouchPoints are the individual moments in time and space when the consumer has an experience with your solution. It happens over an extended period of time. Each time they see, hear, touch, smell, taste or experience your solution, an entry is made on their emotional branding scorecard.

As in most areas of life, it is the accumulative impact of consistent effort that pays dividends and leads to true success. Look at dieting. The enthusiasm offered up by people at the beginning of a diet usually evaporates before any meaningful results are seen. It's the day-in and day-out accumulative effort of eating the right foods and pushing away from the table that gets results.

The same is true of exercise. There's a flurry of activity at health clubs around New Year's every year, but the commitment to work out and get in shape is quickly whittled away by schedules, work and other priorities. When the effort is consistent and accumulates, however, those diets turn plump women into hot babes and flabby guys into hunks.

Branding works the same way. Every time the consumer comes into contact with the solution, emotional connections are made stronger or weaker. Those TouchPoints take place across a wide range of channels. From working with the actual solution, to speaking with a company representative, to receiving a direct mail piece, to making a phone call to the call center, the consumer experiences the branding process in action. Each TouchPoint is important and some will be critical.

Problems occur, of course, and difficulties with the solution don't necessarily spell doom for the branding effort. In fact, some research suggests that a problem corrected successfully creates a stronger sense of loyalty from the customer. The thinking goes that "Since they took care of me when there was a problem, I want to keep using this brand. At least I know they react positively when there is a service issue."

The better the branding effort and the smarter the branding strategy, the more consistent those TouchPoints will be across the channels. Today, contact with customers via the telephone and Web is larger than it's ever been. The efficiency of call centers and the Internet will continue to drive contact with customers to these important TouchPoint channels in years to come.

Definitions

Before we look more closely at brands and branding, let's review their definitions.

Brand (*noun*) **1 a:** a piece of wood that has been or is burning (as one from a hearth or a burning building): **FIREBRAND b:** something that resembles a burning piece of wood <blinding *brands* of lightning — P. B. Shelley>

2 a: a sword blade **b: SWORD**

3 a (1): a mark of a simple easily recognized pattern made by burning with a hot iron to attest manufacture or quality or to designate ownership **(2):** a mark made with a stamp or stencil for similar purposes: **TRADEMARK b (1):** a mark put on criminals with a hot iron **(2):** a mark of disgrace: **STIGMA** <a reputation bearing the *brand* of criminal negligence>

4 a (1): a class of goods identified as being the product of a single firm or manufacturer: **MAKE** <stores selling well-known *brands* of canned foods> **(2): PRODUCER, MANUFACTURER** <a dozen brands of textile goods competing on the open market> **b:** a characteristic or distinctive kind: **VARIETY** <their *brand* of love was a tortured and fretful affection — Evelyn Eaton>

5: a tool used to produce a *brand* (as on cattle, manufactured wares, wine casks): **BRANDING IRON**

6: any rust fungus giving a burnt appearance, typically to leaves

Brand and Branding (*verb*)

1: to mark with a *brand* <brand a criminal> <brand wine casks with the vineyard's name>; especially: to place the *brand* of ownership on (horses or cattle)

> **2:** to mark, signal or expose as being disgraceful or dishonest: **STIGMATIZE** <refusal of such a demand *brands* one as stingy—Margaret Mead>
> **3:** to impress indelibly <history has once again *branded* this lesson on the minds of those who choose to see —T. O. Beachcroft>

As you can see from these *Merriam-Webster Unabridged* definitions, the brand began as a burning piece of wood in a fire. Brand also means "sword" in Old Norse, coming from the Viking and medieval Scandinavians.

The *Landor Dictionary of Branding Terms* has several entries that are of interest:

Term/Definition

Look and Feel: The overall impression created and maintained over time by the consistent presentation of the brand in the prescribed manner and in appropriate contexts.

Brand: The sum of all the characteristics, tangible and intangible, that make the offer unique.

Brand Essence: The distillation of a brand's intrinsic characteristics into a succinct core concept.

Brand Harmonization: The synchronization of all elements of brand identity, across a line of products or services and/or across geographic markets.

Brand Identity: The outward manifestation of the essence of a corporate brand, product brand, service brand or branded environment.

Brand Positioning: The specific niche in which the brand defines itself as occupying in the competitive environment. Positioning addresses differentiating brand attributes, user benefits and target segments, singly or in combination.

Branding: The process by which both a brand and brand identity are developed.

Corporate Brand: The gestalt of the organization, including its philosophy and culture as well as its physical characteristics.

Ingredient Brand: A strong brand that is used and promoted as a key part of a host brand.

Interactive Branding: Process of developing Websites and other interactive products, including strategy development, structural design and graphic design.

Product Brand: Two meanings, both valid: 1) The gestalt of the brand, including its emotional and cultural associations as well as its physical features, and

---

It's interesting to note that the phrase "voice brand" has yet to make it into the dictionaries of most of the leading brand-building experts. Let's check back next year.

The Old West

The Old West is where we get our most common vision of branding. During that time of year when ranchers rounded up their cattle for the drive to the stockyards, the brand on a cow identified its rightful owner. When the push to market reached fevered pitch, many herds merged together on the open range, and a brand on a steer's rear settled many arguments before they happened.

So the first brands established ownership. Since the ranchers were proud of their cattle, they began to make interesting designs with their brands.

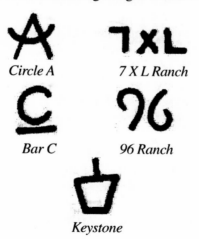

Circle A   *7 X L Ranch*

Bar C   *96 Ranch*

Keystone

Source: Brands: http://memory.loc.gov/ammem/ncrhtml/crview08.html

This article by Marc Simmons in *The Santa Fe New Mexican* provides an interesting historical perspective on branding in the Wild West.

TRAIL DUST: COLORFUL OLD HISPANIC LIVESTOCK BRANDS SAID TO RESEMBLE "GIANT HIEROGLYPHS"

By Marc Simmons, 15 May 2004
Reproduced with permission

The marking of livestock with brands to establish ownership is one of the oldest customs of the ranching industry. In fact, the ancient Egyptians used brands, as can be seen in paintings on walls of their tombs.

The practice of branding was brought from Spain and introduced to Mexico about 1528. Its use was carried northward to the Rio Grande Valley by Governor Juan de Onate and his settlers in 1598.

Branding is performed with a red-hot iron, which burns the hair of an ox, cow, horse or mule. The exposed hide forms an identifying mark on the animal, easily read from a distance.

The design of the brand, created by the owner, was a personal emblem or shield of the ranch and was jealously guarded. Those adopted by Spaniards tended to be large and rather exotic in form.

An American visitor in the 1840s described New Mexico brands he saw as resembling "giant hieroglyphs." A fellow countryman thought they looked like "Chinese characters."

Spanish brands were usually contrived from letters, numerals, geometric figures or even abstract designs. The use of one or more crosses was also commonly seen.

From the earliest days, unscrupulous persons derived various ways of misusing brands in an effort to steal livestock. The Spanish colonial government, in 1574, passed laws that regulated the production and ownership of all branding irons.

Any blacksmith who forged a new iron, not properly registered, might be hauled into court and fined 100 pesos. Still, crooks found means to get around such laws.

Each Franciscan mission in the Spanish Southwest had a separate brand to identify its livestock. Mission San Gabriel near Los Angeles, for instance, came up with an iron formed of a capital T superimposed on the letter S.

The "TS" stood for *temblores* (earthquakes). San Gabriel, because of its unstable location, was known as the Mission of Earthquakes.

People coming from the states were always astonished to see New Mexico's horses and mules wearing a number of different brands. That was owing to the custom of rebranding each time an animal changed hands.

Every local stockman marked increases in his herd with his personal brand, called in Spanish the *fierro*. When it came time to sell a horse, mule or cow, he was required to cancel out his *fierro* by burning another brand underneath the old. This one was called the *venta* or sale brand. Some Americans also referred to the *venta* as a "quit-claim brand." Often it was produced by simply reversing the *fierro*.

A branding iron could be applied to an animal's shoulder, neck or rump. After passing through numerous sales, the beast's hide displayed multiple scars of *fierros* and *ventas*, forming a visible record of successive title deeds.

Josiah Gregg, upon reaching Santa Fe in 1833, observed: "The laws and customs of this country with regard to the ownership of animals are very annoying to the inexperienced foreign traveler."

He was speaking of newly-arrived Easterners who knew nothing about the legal "venting" of brands. Not infrequently, they would buy a horse or saddle mule without the seller's applying his *venta*.

A few days later, the original owner would appear before a magistrate claiming his equine property had been stolen. When the animal was examined and found to lack a *venta*, the magistrate would order it returned to the plaintiff.

William W. H. Davis, attorney for the Territory of New Mexico, noted upon his arrival at the capital in 1853 that the old Hispanic law on branding had recently been altered to do away with the *venta*. "Now," he said, "ownership of livestock is proved in the usual manner," meaning by the issue of a written bill of sale.

American ranchers were soon registering smaller and simpler brands than those used by native New Mexicans. Indeed, the colorful old Hispanic brands, so closely linked to our rural history, shortly faded from the scene.

While the brand was originally meant to determine ownership, it soon began to stand for quality. *If you have the DoubleXX brand, you've got better beef, because our cattle feed on the more succulent grass in our spring-fed meadows.* Communicating your brand's quality is still the pivotal value in branding efforts.

Brand New Industries provides a number of branding solutions today, including this brand used in the White House to brand hamburger buns!

There's one area of branding I believe will be slow to catch on. You're no doubt aware that you can now have any part of your body pierced or tattooed. Those body artists can also provide a personalized "brand" or "burn" of your favorite word or symbol on any spot on your body. I think I'll pass on this one.

Personal Branding

Personal branding is a new way to look at career planning. Did you even realize there are personal branding coaches working out there today? A Google search for "personal branding" returns over 18,000 references. There are branding strategies at the corporate level, product/service level and even personal level. Why? Because in today's difficult corporate climate, many employees feel they are only as secure as their last performance review, and they believe performance often has nothing to do with delivery of a pink slip. There are so many stories today about employees who performed superbly but, because of shenanigans by senior executives and accounting folks, they found themselves looking for work. Or maybe it happened because a merger where "nonessential" or "duplicated" staff members were given "career adjustments" (laid off, terminated or fired).

The dedicated career man or woman is referenced sentimentally because, in what has become a very bottom-line-oriented world, anyone can find themselves out of work. So, as the workplace has become more volatile, smart workers are stepping up to the plate and taking more responsibility for their personal value to the marketplace. That's why you need to learn to manage and promote your personal brand. In a sense, you must continuously increase your value to your current employer through outside training, education and measurable results. At the same time, you are preselling your great value to possible future employers.

Personal Branding (*noun*) Personal branding has not worked its way into *Merriam-Webster* yet. Check back next year.

If you believe that most people are rewarded in some proportion to their value to the organization, you've got to work at building your personal brand in the organization.

You can hire a personal coach to help guide you in your efforts to grow the value of your personal brand, but you can begin by thinking of yourself as a business. One of the main objectives of a business is to generate revenue and profit and thereby increase its value. The same is true with individuals. Today, it's about "You, Inc." or, more appropriately, "Me, Inc."

THE THREE CS OF PERSONAL BRANDING
by William Arruda
Reproduced with permission.

The benefits of being a strong brand are tremendous. As a strong brand, you command higher pay or fees; you thrive during economic downturns; you get to choose the clients, assignments or positions you want; and you can transition your business or career with ease.

In addition to being able to boast these enviable benefits, strong brands have something else in common. They all exhibit the "Three Cs" of branding: clarity, consistency, and constancy. Does your brand pass the Three Cs Test?

CLARITY

Strong brands are clear about who they are and who they are not. They understand their unique promise of value. And this promise of value sets them apart from their competitors. It differentiates them and allows them to attract and build loyalty among the groups of people who can help them achieve their goals.

Richard Branson, for example, is clear about being a risk-taker. He is not your typical CEO in a blue suit and white shirt. He is a daredevil who dressed in a wedding gown when he launched Virgin Bridal, and was not dressed at all when he launched his book, *Virginity*. Among his first big risky ventures was signing the Sex Pistols onto his record label when no one else would even consider them. Since then, Branson has taken on both British Airways with Virgin Airlines, and Coke, the strongest brand in the world, with Virgin Cola.

Even beyond the professional arena, Richard Branson is clear about being a risk-taker. While many CEOs travel the world comfortably in their plush corporate jets, Branson set off to circumnavigate the world in a hot air balloon.

CONSISTENCY

In addition to being clear about who they are, strong brands are also consistent. Madonna is an excellent example of brand consistency. She is the chameleon brand of entertainment. She reinvents herself with each CD she produces.

Now that might seem inconsistent. But in fact, Madonna changes with incredible consistency. She didn't change for her first five CDs and then stay the same for the next two. She consistently changed, each time starting a trend. We know for sure that her upcoming CD will be nothing like any of the others she has done before.

Madonna has her public waiting on the edge of their seats, wondering what will emerge next. Her ability to change consistently throughout her career separates her from other entertainers, thereby strengthening her brand.

CONSTANCY

It is not enough to be clear and consistent if you are not always visible to your target audience. Strong brands are constant. They are always there for their customers and prospects or for those people who can help them achieve their professional goals. American talk show host Oprah Winfrey never goes into hiding. With her weekly television show, her book club, her magazine and her numerous appearances in the media, Oprah is a constant in our lives and an incredibly strong brand. Oprah is the human brand of show biz. She cares for people and is willing to share herself to help people advance. This clarity about what makes her unique is consistent among all of her endeavors. And it is constantly visible to her target audience through her numerous ways of interacting with the public.

Chances are, your brand's target market is a lot smaller than Oprah's. And that is good news, making it easier (and a lot less expensive) for you to remain constantly connected to your target audience.

In uncovering, building and nurturing your brand, you need to keep the Three Cs in mind, because no brand is truly a strong brand if it doesn't pass the Three Cs test. How does your brand do?

William Arruda is the founder of Reach, a global branding company.

Sailing Through a Sea of Brands

The fact is that we are surrounded by brands in everything we do in life. From the moment we wake up in the morning to the moment we lay our heads down to rest at night, we are literally sailing in a sea of brands. From the alarm clock that wakes us to the mattress that takes us to dreamland, brands are everywhere.

Often times we align ourselves with a brand through a silly set of circumstances that we can't even recall. Maybe we choose a particular brand because that's what Mom always used. Maybe it was a recommendation from an acquaintance. Possibly we saw an advertisement on television or stumbled across it in another way.

Look back at the products and services you regularly buy. Pick out a particular brand that you've been buying for years. What was your first connection to it? Why do you reach for it instead of the competing product? Do you remember? In all likelihood, an emotional bond connects you to that brand, and your continued purchases reinforce that relationship one transaction at a time.

Let's spend some time with an average couple down the street: Scott and Sallie. They have three kids—Chelsea is 13, Mandy is 10 and Chase is 7. Scott is 43 and Sallie is 41. They've been married for 15 years. They survived unexpected career changes, a bout of marriage counseling, and some of the other challenges any long union brings to the table. Many of their brand choices are dictated to some degree by their gender and roles. Scott is the main breadwinner of the family and Sallie is the chief homemaker.

We're going to ride shotgun with Sallie for a while to see what brands she chooses and why. Many of them are long-term aids in her life. She's attached to them and wouldn't even consider switching to other products. They've got that emotional connection that most companies would kill for. Then we'll tag along with Scott to learn what brands he decides to invite into his life to help him survive.

Sallie's Brands of Choice

Sallie's a stay-at-home mom except for the parties and events she throws with her part-time Creative Memories business. (Think Longerberger baskets or BeautiControl makeup for the scrapbook crowd.) She's 5' 6" tall and about 130 pounds. Scott insists that she's drop-dead gorgeous because of her genes and her consistent Windsor Pilates workouts. Here's her day:

Beep, beep, beep! The alarm goes off at 5:30 AM. It's a digital Sony clock radio that Scott bought a few years ago. She flips the switch to turn the alarm off and the radio on. It's tuned to a country radio station, WKHX-FM where the brands are musicians: Kenny Chesney, Martina McBride and George Straight.

Now that the music is flowing, Sallie turns on the overhead bedroom light to get her day going. In the bathroom, she brushes her teeth with Crest toothpaste. It was always on the bathroom counter when she was a kid and it followed her into adulthood. She washes her face with Oil of Olay Facial Cleanser and follows up with Nivea moisturizing cream. Her antiperspirant is Secret, "strong enough for a man, but made for a woman."

OK, it's 5:45 AM. She'll need to wake the kids in about 30 minutes. That gives her just enough time to finish the study lesson she's been working on with her community group from church. Her morning "quiet time" is usually about 30 minutes and she cherishes it every day. Sure, sometimes there are interruptions and scheduling problems, but she's made it a priority since college.

It's 6:15 as she heads upstairs for her weekday morning wake-up call. "Everybody up and at 'em," she announces as she turns on the lights in her three kids' rooms. They're awake and will start moving in a few minutes. Now that Chase can get dressed on his own, they can all make it downstairs without a lot of supervision. In about 20 minutes, they'll congregate at the table for breakfast.

In the kitchen, a bevy of brands will be swimming by as Sallie queues up the morning meal. While she remembers everyone eating breakfast at the same time in an orderly fashion when she was a kid, she's given up on making that happen with her kids. It just doesn't work. There are simply too many things happening, too many personalities, and too many agendas. So they march through the kitchen in haphazard order during the 45 minutes between wake-up and bus pickup.

The one consistent thing in Sallie's life is the mix of brands that makes its way to the table. The coffee maker was loaded the night before with Maxwell House from the blue can. (The red Folgers can never makes it into the house for some reason.) There's always orange juice provided by Tropicana. She can't remember why, but that's the brand she's always picked up and the kids seem to like it. Pancakes, waffles and oatmeal are on some sort of rotation, but she can't really predict which is coming up on any particular morning. The pancakes and waffles are courtesy of Bisquick because you just add eggs and milk, and it tastes like made-from-scratch.

Snacks for the kids' lunches vary a good bit. She always makes it a point to include something fresh, usually fruits or vegetables. The packaged snacks include Lay's Potato Chips, "Betcha can't eat just one," or Chee-tos. There's often a peanut butter and jelly sandwich made with Jif Peanut Butter because "choosy moms choose Jif."

The energy level is at its morning peak as all three kids dash out the door to the bus stop at 7:00. They are big enough that Sallie doesn't feel the need to walk them to the stop, although she still goes a couple of days a week just to talk to the other moms. She glances at the stop from the door step and waves good bye.

Now that the morning rush is over, she can take a break with a second cup of coffee. She makes a mini pot this time just for her. Scott likes Maxwell House when he gets up, but Sallie prefers a cup of flavored coffee to help her wind down after the kids leave.

While she's relaxing for a moment with her Millstone Hazelnut coffee, she reaches for the remote control for the small TV on the kitchen cabinet. They dropped the local cable company last year for DirecTV on satellite. It was really Scott's decision because of some sports package. The television is a Toshiba, as are the other three in the house. Click, there's NBC's *Today Show*. From Bryant Gumble and Jane Paley to Matt Lauer and Katie Couric, this has always seemed liker Sallie's spot on the morning television dial. She tried the ABC and CBS efforts, but she just couldn't connect with them.

She needs to get a load of clothes going. It continues to amaze her how much clothing they go through every week. Stepping into the laundry room, she's surprised to see that Mandy has already loaded the washer! She does a quick check on the contents and reaches for the Tide. It's been one of the most consistently purchased brands in the house for almost 16 years. How many boxes has she purchased in that time? Talk about the lifetime value of a customer!

It was an easy generational jump for Sallie to buy Tide because that was the only box in the laundry room when she was a child. When Sallie was six years old, she marched up to her mother and stated emphatically that she was going to start doing the laundry to help out. "I just need you to help me with it," she insisted as she attempted to put her apron on. Mom smiled, then lifted Sallie up and put her on the counter beside the washer. She carefully guided Sallie's hand to the cup that was in the box of Tide, slid it across the top of the detergent, and filled it with the white soap.

Following her loving mother's guidance, Sallie slowly poured the full cup of powder on top of the clothes that were piled high in the washer. To this day, Sallie can still see how the powder sprinkled over the blue jeans and red shirt that were on top. She can see the cup slowly tilting over, her hand in her mom's hand, those white powdery specks flowing out like water. The Tide slid down the little mountains and valleys of the wrinkled clothes. She remembers the water rising in the washer until only a few cloth icebergs broke the surface. That memory is like a wonderful movie she plays in her mind occasionally when she does laundry. Now, when she goes to the store, what detergent is she going to buy?

Back to the kitchen, where she throws the breakfast dishes into the dishwasher. Only takes a couple of minutes. She knows her way around this part of the world. Opening the lower cabinet door under the sink, she pulls out the Cascade dishwashing soap and fills up the little box in the washer door. The phone rings as she shuts the door and presses "Start."

It's Dena on the phone, courtesy of BellSouth. She's calling to confirm their lunch date at Portabella's. It's a sandwich shop near City Hall where they get together at least once a month for their discussion that never ends. Year after year, it just keeps going and going. Yes, she'll be there on time.

It's about 10:15 AM now and Sallie has about an hour before she needs to leave for lunch. She goes to her desk to revisit the To-Do list she made last night. She's actually got a pretty busy day, with several errands, including trips to Chico's, Kroger and Barnes and Noble. She thinks through her order and route to be most efficient. She smiles, thinking, "Wouldn't Scott be proud of me for thinking in a man-like-efficient-motion-studies sort of way?" She'll have to tell him about it later.

Sallie jumps in her Ford Expedition and heads out to Chico's, which is located just across the street from the mall on one of those village-like strip centers. She pulls up and goes in to swap a blouse that a friend gave her as a belated birthday gift. It wasn't the right size. Sallie was a little surprised that her friend thought she was a 12. Doesn't she still look like a 10? She'll have to ask Scott when she gets home. The transaction at Chico's is quick. They had the right size waiting because she'd called about the exchange a couple of days ago.

That was quick. Now she can handle the Barnes and Noble stop before lunch! This is great for a few extra minutes she can use elsewhere. Sallie buys the new John Grisham book for Scott. He really likes Grisham's books. "He's a great storyteller," Scott says after reading each one.

Dena and Karen were already at Portabella's when Sallie arrived. They'd taken their normal good-weather table out on the patio with a view of the park. Dena had just picked up a gift certificate at Edwin Watts Golf for her husband Mike. She pointed out that one of his golfing buddies suggested the gift certificate so he can pick out what he needs. She'd recently learned that he only used Titlest balls after presenting him with a box of Top Flites she had picked up at the discount store.

Karen had found a new lip gloss that was the best she'd ever used: CoverGirl Bronze Ice. The two other women made mental notes to pick up their own tubes a day or two later. Then they talked about stores in the mall that smelled good like The Yankee Candle Company and Bath & Body Works.

After lunch, Sallie moved on to Office Depot to pick up the supplies she needs for the Creative Memories party she's hosting tonight at a new friend's house. She needed name tags, Sharpies, Post-it Notes, copier paper and HP ink cartridges.

OK, back in the car and off to Kroger. Sallie has developed a pretty good system for food shopping. As long as she is purchasing in advance, she'll buy particular items at certain stores. Today she shops the Kroger, Wal-Mart and Super Target triad. She also throws in an every-other-week trip to Sam's Club. All four stores are within a reasonable distance.

She knows lemons, which Scott really likes in his iced tea, are the best value at Sam's Club. She can get an entire bag for a few dollars. At Super Target, the lemons were beautiful and large, but they cost 50¢ each—a bit of a budgetary "ouch!" Since she started shopping with a Texas Instruments calculator a few years ago, she really developed a great system for saving their hard-earned dollars. Kroger is just down the street and is okay for staples such as milk, bread and sandwich fixings. Super Target is good for household cleaning supplies like Windex, Tilex and Comet. On many other things, Wal-Mart and Target are neck-in-neck in the race for low-cost supremacy. Sallie prefers to shop at Target, however, because it's nicer. Sam's is the place for large-quantity items like the 50-bar box of Nature Valley.

Today, it is a quick jaunt to Kroger for ketchup and soft drinks. Scott and Chelsea like Coca-Cola, Mandy prefers Sprite, Chase is a Dr. Pepper man, and Sallie drinks Evian water. She's lessened her commitment to Evian, however, as the water market has become so competitive over the last year or so. Now she also buys Dasani or Aquafina…whichever is within reach.

As Sallie strolls through the aisles carrying the Kroger basket, she picks up Q-tips and Diet Coke, then stops in front of the ketchup display. On the shelf are Heinz, Hunt's and the store brand. No deliberation. It's Heinz. Always has been, always will be.

At the checkout line, things back up a bit. She notices the self-scan line and opts to do it herself. She's gotten used to the self-checkout after several times. She resisted it for about six months until one day the lines at the regular check-outs were way too long. On top of that, all the people in line had their carts filled to the top.

"How hard can it be?" she asked herself as she stepped over to the empty self-checkout line. She only had five or six items that day. She'd never really scanned anything herself, but she'd seen the clerks do it a million times. They just slid it over the little window on the counter, listened for the beep, and watched the purchase amount appear magically on the screen.

That was a couple of months ago. Now she's an old pro at self-checkout. Put the basket on the counter, select the payment method, scan the items, place them in the bag, insert your Visa card and voilá you're done. She's walking out the door before there's any movement in the regular checkout lines. Scott would be proud. He always frets about whether or not he's picking the fastest checkout line.

It's 4:00. The kids will start rolling in any minute. Sallie clicks on the TV to watch Oprah while she prints out the Creative Memories Sell Sheets for tonight's party. Oprah has the kind of content Sallie loves. She likes Dr. Phil too, but won't have time for him today.

Before the kids start arriving, Sallie calls for pizza. They were a Domino's family for many years, but they switched to Papa John's last year and were pleased with the change. The bread sticks are a real treat for Chase, and one large pizza is enough for the entire family. She has plenty of Coke, Sprite and Dr. Pepper for drinks. She's also got Capri Suns in the fridge. Chase likes them because he can stick the little pointed straw in the top and not worry about spillage. No home-cooked meal tonight, which is normal on the nights she hosts a party.

Sallie then strolls through the den and down the hall into the master bedroom on the main floor. When they first started looking to step up to a larger house six years ago, Scott wisely insisted that the master had to be on the main floor and the kids had to be upstairs. It was her second-favorite room when they looked at the house.

She has all her clothes ready. Her new Chico's blouse is on the Ethan Allen chest that serves as an island in the center of the large walk-in closet at the far end of the bedroom. She already has a nice Donna Karan skirt that matches it and a Liz Claiborne belt and purse. Last, but certainly not least, a pair of Nine West sandals with half-inch heels.

Now for a quick shower. The Moen showerhead spurts out nonbranded water from the local municipality as soon as Sallie turns it on. It takes about 60 seconds for the hot water to make its way through the pipes from the Rheem water heater.

Sallie keeps an entire family of brands ready to help her feel clean and beautiful in the bathroom. From hair care and skin products to makeup and fragrances, she knows her favorite brands: Aveda, Bath & Body Works, BeautiControl, Biolage, Caswell Massey, Clinique, Estée Lauder, Dove, Lancôme, Logics, Paul Mitchell, Secret and more.

Now back to the closet where she slips into her clothes and puts on the DeBeers diamond earrings that Scott got for her last birthday. She sprays a little Halston in the air in front of her and walks into the mist floating about neck high. Scott loves this aroma.

Sallie walks back into the kitchen/great room, her favorite room in the house. This is the room she really fell in love with because the kitchen is where real life happens. As a kid growing up, she and her family always gathered, talked, laughed and cried in the kitchen. And this one has a beautiful feel about it as it opens up into a two-story great room.

It's filled with Whirlpool appliances, including a microwave oven that's popped a thousand bags of corn. There's also a large KitchenAid mixer that she needs to put away. She uses it to make the "best banana bread on earth," according to Scott. There's also a Black & Decker toaster oven and a Mr. Coffee morning java machine.

As she rounds the corner on the island, Sallie sees that the kids are home. Chase is rooting around in the pantry for a snack. "Stop that, I ordered a pizza. It'll be here any minute," she says as she gives him a hug. A "Hi, Mom" is mumbled by Mandy, who's at the kitchen table, already working on her algebra homework. Chelsea's on the phone with who knows who. She dutifully kisses them both on the head to avoid interrupting them from anything important.

Sallie looks at the clock. It's 5:30 and Scott's at the door. No, that's the pizza guy. Where is Scott? Suddenly the phone rings. Scott is running a few minutes late. He always tries to get home by 5:30 when he's in town, but sometimes work jumps onto the calendar. Sallie's got a theory she needles Scott with every now and then. She asserts that work, sports and golf are ingredients in a three-part conspiracy to keep men away from their families! Well, he'll show up soon enough.

She pauses for a minute to look over her two rolling suitcases where keeps her Creative Memories materials. Everything looks in order there. When Scott walks in, there's a flurry of activity, with hugs for the kids and a kiss for Sallie. Chelsea fixes the iced tea, Mandy sets the table, and Chase brings the pizza to the table. The motion only stops long enough for a quiet prayer in thanks to God for the great pizza. Everyone sits down for a few minutes as a family.

Over the next 20 minutes or so, as the pizza is wolfed down, a few jokes and stories are bandied about. One tale gets Scott so tickled that he almost chokes, which makes it all the funnier. Soon Chelsea is off to soccer practice with neighbors, Mandy's practicing on the Yamaha piano, and Chase is watching TV. Scott has a couple of emails to send from the home office and Sallie's out the door to her party. It's a busy place, but they wouldn't have it any other way.

The party goes according to plan. She's been doing these parties for two years and has six reps working under her guidance. It's actually grown into a nice income, and the flexibility provides lots of options. Tonight's party becomes her third highest grossing event. She used her big finish at the close of the get-together when she broke out the Godiva chocolates. They are expensive, but oh so good! She always leaves with two or three party guests asking her to do a party in their homes. That's working the network!

When she gets home, she's pretty tired. Scott is reading Tom Clancy's book in the small study nestled in the corner of the master bedroom. She walks over and gives him a hug and kiss. "I can't wait to get in bed," she says as she slowly reveals the black silk Victoria's Secret nightie she's about to change into. It brushes his arm on the La-Z-Boy recliner. She winks at him and walks toward the closet to change.

Scott's interest in his book wanes quickly as his attention moves to Sallie. He puts the book on the small table and walks over to the bathroom. He turns back the Pottery Barn bedspread and jumps into the Charles P. Rogers iron king bed with its Sealy Posturepedic semi-firm mattress. As Sallie eases into the bedroom in her slinky new gown, Scott slowly lowers the lights with his mood-enhancing SwitchLinc remote control dimmer switch. The light gets lower and lower as she approaches the bed. Then the lights go out!

Now, if you're a man, you're probably thinking, "Boy, this Sallie is awesome. If she and Scott split up for some reason, I'd like to ask her out!" If you're a woman, you're probably thinking, "This is a fairy tale. Nobody's that together!"

Scott's Brands of Choice

Now let's ride shotgun with Scott as he goes through his day to see what type of brands he chooses to help make his life easier and more rewarding.

At 43, Scott is Vice President of Business Development for one of the technology companies that survived the Internet and telecom downturn a few years ago. It was a difficult time, but the company hunkered down and came out of it stronger and smarter. Feedback Networks creates software that allows companies to manage feedback from their customers more effectively. It's a web-based solution that lets customers submit requests for new features in the next software release.

He travels about 50% the time, knows sports as well as any man, works out three times a week no matter where he is, and shoots in the 80s at least once a week with customers and friends.

When the alarm goes off, Sallie gets up quickly, but Scott requires more of a "merging awakening" process, as he likes to explain it to her. After about 15 minutes of "thinking" about his day, he gets up and on with his day.

He's a quick shower artist, boasting the ability to take a full shower in three minutes if he's really pressed. He shaves with his Gillette Mach III because three blades must be better than two, right? He noticed recently that Schick has introduced the four-blade Quattro. Guess that means Gillette will have to introduce a five-bladed razor, right?

On occasion, he trims his beard with a Remington trimmer. He uses the same Old Spice deodorant that his dad and grandfather used, so it must be some kind of family tradition. Neither ancestor used mousse, but Scott started using Paul Mitchell mousse recently, after years of encouragement from Sallie. "Don't be afraid of the mousse," Sallie would kid him. He finally came around, and he actually likes it now.

Today, he's got a few things happening before he jumps on a plane for a client meeting in Dallas. His main objective is to close the Carlson deal at lunch. Everything's queued up and the agreements are ready for the client's signature. Scott's been nurturing this deal for about seven months. He'll have to get his bags packed now so he can leave for the airport after lunch.

Even though the business world has become much more casual over the past few years, Scott still wears smart business suits when calling on new clients. He has two: an Armani and a Hugo Boss. He purchases most of his shirts from Nordstrom or Paul Fredrick. He likes Ferragamo shoes, Calvin Klein underwear and Jerry Garcia ties.

With the change to more casual work attire, he typically wears a sport coat and slacks when not meeting with clients. He likes casual shirts from Polo/Ralph Lauren, Cutter & Buck and the golf courses he plays while traveling. He has several watches: a nice Seiko Lasalle that's thin and svelte, a Fossil casual that goes with just about anything, and a Timex Ironman Triathlon sports watch for tracking his running times.

He talks Chase into running out to the driveway and picking up the two newspapers he reads most every day—the daily local and *The Wall Street Journal*. He pours himself a coffee, grabs the bowl of oatmeal that Sallie has waiting, and pulls up a chair to the island bar. Chase delivers his papers a few moments later and he digs into the news. He's up to speed on the world's activities and pays particular attention to the business section. In addition, he gets *Fortune*, the local weekly business journal and half a dozen trade industry publications.

There's always a flurry of morning activity before the kids race to the bus and he enjoys being in the middle of it. Practically speaking, he doesn't really help the process. He's joking with the kids, asking about homework, and being a bit of a pest in a fun sort of way. After skimming the *WSJ*, he collects a couple of client folders and his laptop. He gives each of the kids his customary kiss on the forehead and walks out the garage door.

He gets in the Lexus LS 400 that he bought three years ago. His Cingular cell phone vibrates in his pocket as he pulls out of the driveway. Scott keeps it on vibrate because he hates being interrupted in meetings by those ringing tunes so many people use. It's Janet, his counterpart at a company they partner with in several vertical markets. She's got an opportunity to discuss. They spend about five minutes on it and set up a time to drill down in more detail tomorrow. His commute is easy by most standards—only 12 miles and against the largest flow of traffic headed into the city.

When he gets to the office, Scott turns on his Dell desktop workstation. The 45-person company buys Dell exclusively. Fortunately, Scott doesn't really have to deal with purchasing anything of consequence at the office. He just gets to make a lot of noise when it doesn't work right. He uses a Palm PDA to manage his calendar and contacts—just pops it in the cradle and it synchronizes with Microsoft Outlook whenever he's in the office. He books a flight at www.delta.com for an upcoming trip. Those Sky Miles continue to add up and that's a good thing.

He meets a customer at Chili's for lunch to finalize their agreement. They complete the contract and the new customer signs it using the Monteblanc pen Scott slides across the table with the agreement. Leaving the restaurant, he has an extra pep in his step. He always gets excited when he closes a deal.

Next he's off to Edwin Watts Golf to pick up a new Mizuno lob wedge, some Titleist balls and a new FootJoy golf glove. He stops at the cigar store in the same shopping center for a few Romeo y Julieta cigars for his Friday outing.

Just down the street, he pulls into the Chevron station he regularly uses. He's still got a quarter of a tank, but decides to go ahead and fill it up. He pays at the pump.

His flight to Dallas is at 3:05 PM. He checks in using the new Delta self-serve kiosk near the ticket counter. It's much simpler than waiting in line for a ticket agent. He gets the upgrade he was hoping for. As a Gold Medallion member, he rides in first class about 75% of the time. There are perks to so much travel.

Arrival in Dallas is on time. Because he's a Preferred Club member, his car is ready and waiting at Avis. He heads for West End, where an old college buddy is meeting him for drinks and dinner. About 40 minutes later, he pulls up at The Palms restaurant and the valet takes his car.

Tony's already there. They order a couple of Black and Tans, a drink for the beer connoisseur. It's half Guinness and half Bass Ale. They talk old times and get caught up on current events. Tony's a stockbroker, and he's suggesting that Scott look at a couple of new high-growth opportunities in the marketplace. Scott makes a note to review them on his E*Trade account when he gets home.

After dinner, he heads to the hotel he booked online last week when he planned the trip: the Marriott Courtyard at Market Center. It's just a few miles from his appointment in the morning. He checks in, then spends a few minutes online checking email. He also checks the HBO schedule, but doesn't see anything he wants to watch. He gives Sallie a call to check in and say good night, and it's time for lights out!

As you can see, Scott and Sallie use many brands. We're all surrounded by brands that we know and trust to make our lives easier. The reasons we tend to settle with a particular brand vary greatly. Whether Mom and Dad used it, a friend introduced us to it, we saw it in an advertisement, or we stumbled on it ourselves, we tend to forge relationships with the products and services we buy.

Trademarks

Brands and trademarks are closely related. A trademark issued by the United States Trade and Patent Office establishes that the brand and the components used to communicate it are owned by a particular entity, such as a person or corporation.

Using marks to identify who owns something or who made it goes back thousands of years. According to scholars, paintings of bison on the walls of the Lascaux Caves in southern France contain specific marks that show ownership dating back to 5,000 BC. In 1266, the Bakers Marking Law was passed in England. This law provided guidelines on using identifying stamps or pinpricks on loaves of bread.

Here's the trusty *Merriam-Webster* definition:

Trademark (*noun*)

1: a word, letter, device, sound, symbol, or some combination of these that is used in connection with merchandise, distinctly points inherently or by association to the not-necessarily-known origin or ownership of that to which it is applied, and is legally reserved for the exclusive use of the owner according to statutory provisions: a name or symbol used by a maker or seller to identify distinctively his products <must display his trademark on his product for it to be legally valid> <a *trademark* can only be transferred in connection with the goodwill of the business—Edward Jenks>—compare **COPYRIGHT, SERVICE MARK**

2: a distinctive feature, characteristic or eccentricity that becomes so associated with a person or thing as to be a sign or designation of that person or thing: an identifying mark or feature <the derringers ... became almost a *trademark* of gamblers — Elmer Keith>

Trademark (*verb*)

1: to put or affix a trademark upon: label with a trademark

2: to secure trademark rights for: to register the trademark of

The intellectual property law firm of Beck & Tysver, PLLC., in Minneapolis provides a good overview of trademark devices and how they're employed:

EXAMPLE TRADEMARK DEVICES

June 2, 2004, www.bitlaw.com/trademark/devices.html#sound
Beck & Tysver, PLLC
2900 Thomas Ave South, Suite 100
Minneapolis, MN 55419

Executive Summary: A trademark is a device that can take almost any form, as long as it is capable of identifying and distinguishing specific goods or services. The best way to understand the types of devices available is through actual examples. The examples on this page are divided as follows:

- Letters and Words
- Logos
- Pictures
- Combination of Words and a Logo
- Slogans
- Colors
- Product Shapes
- Sounds

A *word* or other grouping of letters is the most common type of mark. Examples include:

- Apple
- Silicon Graphics
- Netscape
- IBM

Logos are probably the next most common form of mark. A logo can be described as a design that becomes a mark when used in close association with the goods or services being marketed. The logo mark does not need to be elaborate; it need only distinguish goods and services sold under the mark from other goods and services. Examples of logo marks are:

- McDonald's double arches

- NBC's peacock design
- Apple Computer's Apple

Pictures or drawings of a character or scene are often used as trademarks or service marks:
- Apple's discontinued Cyberdog
- Corning's Pink Panther
- Sun Microcomputer, Inc.'s Duke

Or a *trademark* might be a combination of letters and a design, such as: IBM's striped type, Sun Microsystems' monogram and name, and Digital's type aligned in vertical blocks.

Slogans from advertising campaigns are also used as trademarks. Example slogans that have strong trademark rights attached to them are:
- "Where do you want to go today?" (Microsoft)
- "Solutions for a small planet" (IBM)

The *color* of an item can also function as a trademark. The Supreme Court held in the case of *Qualitex Co. v. Jacobson Products Co.*, 115 S. Ct. 1300 (1995), that the green-gold color of a dry cleaning press pad can function as a trademark. Before this decision, the argument was often made that color alone could not be considered a trademark, since granting trademark status to colors would soon lead to the depletion of the number of colors available for an object. The Court in *Qualitex* rejected arguments based on this depletion theory, reasoning that alternative colors would usually be available for competitors. In those cases where alternative colors were not available, courts could deny trademark protection in those circumstances where color depletion may actually occur.

In order for a color to be considered a trademark, the owner must show that secondary meaning has been developed for the color. In addition, a color cannot be a trademark if the color is functional in nature. For example, one court has held that the color black serves a functional purpose when used on outboard boat motors since the color black matches all other boat colors and also makes the motor appear smaller. A second court, however, has stated that it is possible for a color to function as a trademark even if the color contributes to the utilitarian or aesthetic function of a product. A second example of a color mark is the color pink for Owens-Corning's fiberglass insulation.

A *product or container shape* can also serve a source-identifying function and therefore can be an enforceable trademark. A product or container shape may also be subject to a design patent (see the BitLaw discussion of design patents see an analysis of the similarities and differences between design patents and trademark protection for product shapes). Historically, trademark protection was not granted to product shapes until the consuming public recognized the shape as indicating the source of the product. In other words, the product shape was required to obtain secondary meaning. However, recent court decisions may mean that an inherently distinctive product shape can be a protectable trademark even before secondary meaning is obtained.

The prototypical example of a product shape trademark is the Coca-Cola familiar curvy Coca-Cola bottle.

Another notable area of trademark protection is that of *sound.* NBC's three-toned audio logo and MGM's lion roar are trademarked.

On February 1, 1994, Harley-Davidson filed a registration for a trademark with the following description:

"The Mark consists of the exhaust sound of applicant's motorcycles, produced by V-twin, common crankpin motorcycle engines when the goods are in use."

The Harley-Davidson position was that other motorcycle manufacturers were trying to duplicate the unique sound of a Harley, which is inextricably woven within its brand. Their attorney noted that the design results in a syncopated, uneven idle, which, when simulated verbally, sounds like "potato-potato-potato."

Voice Branding

When I first started talking about voice branding in the mid-1990s, the audience wasn't exactly hot on the topic. I'd speak at communications, computer telephony and user conferences about the importance of supporting your organization's brand with a consistent voice. Most of the prerecorded voices on enterprise phone systems at the time were provided by a collection of employees (some former, some current), technology provider staff, or message-on-hold companies.

The audiences then were more on the technical side—from the telecom, voice mail administration or information technology departments. They thought voice branding was interesting and might warrant a little golf clap, but when it was time to get back to work, it was not on their agenda. I kept talking about it and talking about it.

Well, as they say, timing is everything. As speech recognition technology continued to grow and prove itself a strategic tool in lowering costs and improving customer service, the subject of branding began to bubble up in the speech implementation process. Because speech was proving to be a strategic force in many corporations, C-level executives became more involved in the decisions to deploy speech. These executives were already spending millions branding their companies and products every year, so it was easy for them to see the value. They quickly jumped on board because it made good business sense.

Voice User Interface Designers

A lot of the credit for raising the issue of branding in speech recognition belongs to the creative teams at Nuance and SpeechWorks (now ScanSoft). The design professionals at these companies worked on well thought out "personalities" or "personas." They knew in their collective souls that, to make a meaningful and ongoing connection with the caller, the persona had to be reasonable, pleasant and consistent. Of course, the technology had to work, and it works incredibly well today. The user, however, is not concerned with the underlying infrastructure, recognizers, vocabularies, algorithms and all that techno-talk. They just want to conduct their business and be on their way.

The UI professionals at these leading companies sold' their clients and they sold their upper management on the value of getting the prerecorded voice greetings and prompts right. And much like the Broadway performers who transferred their entertainment skills to radio drama, the UI pros applied general design strategies and a touch of Hollywood to the new medium of speech recognition.

ScanSoft Creative Director Blade Kotelly, who helped create the Wildfire Communications persona with an attitude in the early 90s, has been talking about the importance of branding as part of the user interface design for some time. In his book, *The Art and Business of Speech Recognition: Creating the Noble Voice*, he points out the importance of extending the brand to the telephone:

"Most companies pay a great deal of attention to how their brands are communicated in their advertising and marketing literature. But these are outbound communications with no direct, interactive connection to the customer. An advertisement can be ignored or turned off. A brochure can be left unread. But when a customer calls a company, it is one of the most direct and personal contacts that company will ever have with a customer.

"By taking branding into consideration from the beginning, companies can ensure that their phone system handles customers the right way all the time—in a manner that's consistent with its brand identity."

Michael Cohen, who cofounded Nunace in 1994, and his associates James P. Giangola and Jennifer Balogh, recognized the power of the brand in speech recognition, too. In their book, *Voice User Interface Design*, the impact of the brand takes a similar focus:

"Many companies spend large sums on branding and building a corporate image through advertising and other marketing efforts. Brand and corporate image are also projected via a persona, whether or not the persona has been explicitly designed. The persona chosen for a particular application should at least be compatible with brand and corporate identity, if not a chief conveyor of these ideals. The persona must coordinate with any existing brand the company has, as well as with other customer touchpoints."

Which came first, the "persona" or the "voice brand?" General Magic was an early and substantial contributor to the concept of creating a persona. Their groundbreaking persona work in the General Motors OnStar Virtual Advisor product was well received. They even obtained a U.S. patent for a "Voice User Interface with Personality." A number of companies, including GM Voices, felt the patent was not enforceable. It was not a real issue, however, as the company had difficulty translating innovative technological achievements into commercial success and declared bankruptcy in late 2002.

The Voice Brand

The voice brand is that unique combination of voice talent, words, call flow, music, sounds effects, technology and spirit that greets and guides callers. It's largely experienced over the telephone today, but that's changing. With the telephone, computer and television morphing into similar multifunction devices due to digital convergence, a company's voice brand is being heard on websites, multimedia CD ROMs, kiosks, cards, point-of-purchase devices, and who knows what else.

Here are some of the channels where a customer might hear your company's voice brand today:

Technology
- Automated attendants
- Automatic call distributors (ACD)
- Interactive voice response (IVR)
- Intercept messages
- On-hold messages
- Outbound messages notification

- Phone systems
- Private branch exchanges (PBX)
- Speech recognition systems
- Websites

Where
- Call centers
- Local offices
- Partner offices
- Departments

Today, most companies have a hodge-podge of communications technology in their organizations. In addition to a broad collection of technologies and manufacturers, there can be dozens of suppliers who provide these solutions.

The customer, however, is not, and should not be, aware of this mix of equipment that answers the phone call. They are doing business with one company. The experience of the voice brand should offer a sense of consistency to the customer. Too many companies have systems with a schizophrenic multiple personality and a different prerecorded voice on every piece of communication equipment. This confuses the overall brand.

If a brand is built one contact or one customer TouchPoint at a time, those prerecorded voices are playing a big part in building brands in America. Prospects, customers, partners and employees know the company's brand that's been crafted and shaped for years in other media. Does the voice brand support it?

Broader than Speech Recognition

While the people in speech have helped raise the profile, voice branding is much broader than speech recognition. Although most speech applications are deep in persona quality, they represent a small part of the voice brand throughout the enterprise. A company's voice brand is out there greeting and speaking to thousands, tens of thousands, of customers every day.

If voice branding is a sea, there's usually only one application that is reaching "deep" on the voice branding quality scale-speech recognition. Most of the other customer TouchPoints present a wide range of quality to customers. They are "shallow" on the scale.

	Auto Attendant	Voice Mail	After-hours	ACD Queing	IVR	Speech Reco	On-Hold Message	Website	Mobile Agents
Shallow									
Deep									

(Voice Branding Quality Scale shown on vertical axis, from Shallow to Deep)

Technology Rat's Nest

From a technology standpoint, it's cluttered. Let's look at WidgetCo's operation to see where the voice brand can be found, what technology is being used and which companies are supplying it. WidgetCo has 164 remote sales locations around the country. There are two ACDs and two IVRs in the contact centers, 175 message-on-hold systems, a narrated audio guide on a portion of the Website, and a after-hours voice mailbox in every location and every department in the company.

WidgetCo Telecom Matrix

Locations	Technology	Providers
Remote Sales Offices, 164	Nortel Norstar Switches, 47	Different Resellers, 16
Call Centers, 2	Lucent Partner PBX 62	Different Resellers, 9
Regional Ops Centers, 11	Aspect Call Center ACD, 2	Aspect Direct, 1
	IVR, 2	Edify Direct, 1
	Speech Recognition, 2	Interalia, 60
	Message-on-hold, 175	Premiere Tech, 39

As noted in the example above, there are simply too many components, too many locations and too many providers. There are too many parts to this puzzle for anyone to get excited about putting it together.

Creating and Managing Your Voice Brand

Voice Brand Audit

Decisions about telephone messages and the image they project rarely make it to the chief marketing officer's radar screen, even though millions of customers are subjected to them every year. The owners of the "brand" don't have the tools to affect an enterprise-wide voice-branding initiative.

So the reason "brand" owners weren't including voice branding in their marketing plans was that they can't quantify it. Executives would usually call in like customers. If they did hear an isolated automated attendant or IVR greeting, what would that tell them?

"We knew there was a problem with the image and message we were sending on our automated voice systems, but we couldn't figure out how to address it."
— Fortune 1000 Marketing Executive

We knew we had to create a solution that allowed them to look at the voice brand strategically. That's when GM Voices teamed up with Siemens' Senior Sales Manager Mark Daley to create an interactive CD ROM for their customers that documented their voice brands across a wide range of technology.

The GM Voices creative staff called dozens of prospective customer phone numbers in secret shopper mode and recorded their current call handling process. The actual phone calls were edited and placed on a CD ROM that allowed executives to quickly hear their voice brand and call handling process in action across many locations and departments. It showed a level of customer intimacy and knowledge that helped them win more sales.

We now call them TouchPoint Reports. They usually serve as the starting point of any viable enterprise-wide voice branding initiative.

Voice Branding Project Methodology

Any enterprise-wide initiative has risks associated with it. What if it doesn't work out as planned? What happens if the implementation stalls? The process is king in a voice branding initiative. It's about dotting I's and crossing T's. As a frame of reference, here's the actual persona/voice branding project methodology we use at GM Voices.

GM Voices Persona/ Voice Branding Project Methodology

1. Requirements
    a. Business Requirements
    b. User Needs and Requirements
    c. Application Requirements
    d. Persona Requirements
    e. Branding Requirements
    f. Demographics and Target Market Identification
    g. Knowledge of Expectations (both client and GMV)

    h. Knowledge of Existing Systems, Manufacturers, Locations and Voicing Capabilities (TouchPoints Report)

2. Voice Brand Audit
   a. TouchPoints Report CD ROM
   b. Company Structure
   c. Departments/Locations Identification
   d. Calling Criteria
   e. Generation and Recording of Calls
   f. Brainstorming Session

3. Design
   a. Develop Persona and Voice Branding
   b. Work with VUI Designer and App Developer for Dialogue Design/Call Flow
   c. Record Audio files for Prototype System
   d. Use Professional Voice Talent and Persona (if appropriate — would require selection of voice talent during design phase)
   e. Develop Nonspeech Audio (Earcons, Music and Branding)
   f. Evaluate Persona (may be part of iterative usability and/or client meetings)

4. Audio Production
   a. Voice Talent Selection
       i. Present Voice Actor Sample Prompts
       ii. Get Approval from Selection Committee
       iii. Receive Order via Electronic Order Form (EOF)
   b. Studio-Ready Script Preparation
   c. Persona and Voice Production
       i. Recording Session
       ii. Voice Talent Coaching
   d. Audio Delivery
       i. Editing
       ii. Digitizing
       iii. Formatting
       iv. Quality Assurance Testing of Finished Voice Prompts
       v. Delivery of Ready-to-Load Prompts via FTP and Provision of Backup CDROM

  e. Audio Production steps are typically concurrent with Application Implementation and Grammar Development

5. Ongoing Maintenance
  a. Audio Testing (Work with VUI Designer and App Developer)
    i. Application Testing
    ii. Dialogue Testing
    iii. Speech Recognition Testing
    iv. Usability Testing
  b. Audio Updates and Revisions
    i. Archive Voice Prompts and Match Updates to Initial Project Recordings
    ii. Receive Orders via EOF
    iii. Provide Ongoing Voice Prompt Updates and Revisions
    iv. Fine-tune to Optimize New Voicing, Record Revisions if Necessary

After-Hours Info Center

One of the fastest ways to pay for a voice brand audit, is to include an After-Hours Info Center in the final action plan. During business hours, your system greets callers and addresses their needs, but what about calls that come in after hours? What happens then? In most companies, the after-hours caller hears the receptionist or call center rep saying, "Thanks for calling. Leave a message and we'll call you back on the next business day." That's nuts. What if the customer hangs up and calls your competitor—the one who does have a powerful after-hours info center? By neglecting these customers, you dramatically increase the chance that they will call and/or buy from a competitor. Either way, you lose.

A simple After-Hours Info Center with a strong, creative tie to your brand can give every prospect compelling reasons to buy from you. It will eliminate even the consideration of their looking at another provider. With the right call flow, script, voice actor and audio assets, you can turn this prospect into a long-term customer. Here's what it would looks like with our sample company, WidgetCo.

Auto Attendant Sample Script

Day Greeting: Thank you for calling WidgetCo, the world's largest widget solution provider. If you know your party's extension, enter it now. For an operator, press 0 at any time.

Night Greeting:	Thank you for calling WidgetCo, the world's largest widget solution provider. We're open Monday through Friday from 8 AM to 6 PM. But please don't hang up! We may still be able to help you with our After-Hours Information Center. If you know your party's extension, enter it now. For an operator, press 0 at any time.
Main Menu:	For the sales department, press 1. For the service department, press 2. For the accounting department, press 3. To learn why WidgetCo should be your widget provider, press 4. To hear what our customers have to say about us, press 5. For the Operator, press 0.
Why WidgetCo:	WidgetCo is the world's leading provider of high-quality widgets. In fact, our innovative production techniques and rigorous quality controls set the industry standard for widgets. We offer a wide variety of sturdy, reliable widgets, gimbels, whozits and plinkers, always in stock and shipped the same day you order. Need a widget for thermal applicators? Ask your WidgetCo representative about our new heat-resistant widgets, tested to 150 degrees Farenheit. You can download our catalog at W W W dot WidgetCo dot com. And remember: On-site consultation by an authorized WidgetCo representative is available at no charge. WidgetCo—Can you really afford to settle for less?
Testimonials:	Rick Jones, Operations Director "My experience with WidgetCo has been very good. Their reps know their industry and I can rely on them for a recommendation on the right product that best fits what I need." Janice Rodgers, Vice President: "WidgetCo's products work very well compared to those of their competitors. The fit is always correct and we've never had any problem with downtime because of broken widgets."

Tom Barnes, Vice President:
"We've tried other, cheaper widgets and know from experience that's not the way to go. You truly get what you pay for, and with WidgetCo, you're getting the best product in the industry."

Operator: Leave your message now in the General Delivery mailbox. We'll return your call on the next business day.

Take careful note of what happens on every after-hours call. The caller is presented with the opportunity to learn more about your solutions. The information is presented in a very powerful manner when your customers tell why they love working with you in their own voices. They have been interviewed and recorded by phone. Those sound bites become strong sales presentations in your After-Hours Info Center. You can even put them on your website or on-hold programs. There is no better spokesperson for your company than satisfied customers—they've got credibility.

Ironically, this is very inexpensive to do. You already have the voice mail system or service. An administrator simply adds a few mailboxes to the application. It's a no-brainer. So what happens when we call *your* company after-hours?

Request for Proposal (RFP)

While Requests for Proposal (RFPs) are a lot of work, they are a great way to develop a good understanding of a process that may be new to you. If you'd like to receive an electronic copy of a Voice Branding Initiative RFP, please visit the GM Voices website or contact your account manager. With dozens of questions, the answers will provide a detailed framework for managing a voice branding initiative. You may need to change it a bit for your organization, but it will save a ton of time.

Voice Branding Initiative RFP Form
   1) Introduction
   2) Executive Summary
   3) Vendor Profile and Capabilities
   4) Financial Info
   5) References
   6) Clients

7) Partners/Third Parties

8) Core Competencies

9) Voice Branding

10) Languages/International

11) Voice File Specifications

12) Order Submission

13) Delivery Turnaround Times

14) Ongoing Maintenance

15) Industry Experience

16) Project Methodology and Improvement

17) Nonverbal Audio

18) Pricing

19) PSA/SLA

20) Glossary of Terms

PART II: PRERECORDED VOICES

The definition of "voice" in "voice branding" is much broader than the voice talent's vocal sounds. *Merriam-Webster Unabridged Dictionary* has seven definitions of the noun "voice" and four definitions of the verb "voice." None of them really hits the mark in defining "voice branding," but some do serve as a good frame of reference.

Voice (*noun*) Etymology: Middle English voice, vois, from Old French vois, voiz, from Latin voc-, vox

1 a: sound produced by vertebrates by means of lungs, larynx or syrinx, and various buccal structures <the chorused voices of the birds>; especially: sound so produced by human beings (as in speaking, singing, crying or shouting) **b** (1): the musical sound produced by the vocal cords and resonated by the various cavities of head and throat and differing chiefly from voice in speaking in the greater prolongation of vowel sounds on definite pitches (2): the power or ability to produce musical tones <have a voice> <train the voice> (3): **SINGER** <the great voices of an age> (4): also **VOICE PART:** one of the melodic parts in a vocal or instrumental composition <the bass voice of a fugue> (5): condition of the vocal organs with respect to the production of especially musical tones <be in good voice> (6): the use of the voice in singing, acting, public speaking <study voice> <classes in voice> **c:** expiration of air with the vocal cords drawn close so as to vibrate audibly (as in uttering vowels and such consonant sounds as \v\ or \z\)-compare BREATH VOICELESS, WHISPER **d:** the organs by which uttered sound is produced <strained her voice with coughing> **e:** the faculty or power of utterance: SPEECH <fear took away his voice>

2 a: characteristic sound produced by animals using other than vocal mechanisms (as stridulation) <cheerful voice of the cricket> **b:** a sound resembling or suggesting vocal utterance <distant voice of a waterfall> <silvery voices of bells> <hoarse voice of a foghorn> <wailing voices of sirens>

3: something resembling human speech in being an instrument or medium of expression <majestic voice of the law> <voice of conservatism>

4 a: wish, choice, or opinion openly or formally expressed <policy adopted despite many dissenting voices> **b:** the right to express a wish, choice or opinion: **SAY, SUFFRAGE** <every member of the family had a voice in making the plan>

5: obsolete: RUMOR, FAME

6: one that speaks: one that warns, urges, prompts or commands <guided by an inner voice> <ancestral voices prophesying war — S.T. Coleridge> <voice of doom> <saw visions and heard voices>

7: distinction of form or a particular system of inflections of a verb to indicate the relation of the subject of the verb to the action which the verb expresses

Voice (*verb*)

1 a: to give utterance to: **UTTER** <a chance to voice his objections> <has voiced the sentiments of the whole group> **b** obsolete: REPORT, RUMOR

2: obsolete: to appoint by or as if by voting: ELECT

3: to adjust for producing the proper musical sounds: regulate the tone of <to voice the pipes of an organ>

4: to utter with sonant or vocal tone produced by vibration of the vocal cords: pronounce with voice <the vowels and such consonants as \b\, \v\, \j\ are voiced in contrast with \p\, \f\, \ch\>

intransitive verb: to pronounce a sound with voice

Most of the definitions are focused on the actual voice speaking, uttering or otherwise performing a script. There is no doubt the voice talent is a very important part of the message heard on an automated application and that it has a major impact on the user. In our more expansive view, however, "voice" means everything about the communication.

The broader voice includes a dozen or more considerations outside of the physical voice: the company's personality, the application, the audience, the script, the call flow, the attitude, the intonation, the inflection, the prosody, the meaning, the nonverbal audio. It's the sound embodiment of the entire brand. The actual spoken voice is really the tip of the iceberg. As you know, only a small part of an iceberg is visible above the waterline. Perhaps only ten percent can be seen. The majority of it is hidden below the surface and out of sight. Just like the impact of your voice brand.

We've been hearing anonymous voices for decades in radio and television. In the early days, those voices were live. Eventually, those messages were created in the studio and saved on magnetic recording tape. This allowed producers and advertisers to control the consistency of their message and expand the level of complexity in their programs.

Today, there are millions of prerecorded messages played to callers over the phone. From network intercept and call center delay messages to IVR voice prompts and speech recognition applications, the sheer volume of information shared via prerecorded voice messages is staggering.

And the number of places and applications that prerecorded voices are used is exploding. Here are just a few that are commonplace today:

• Amusement parks	• Gas stations	• Public areas
• ATMs	• Interactive games	• Radio
• Automobiles	• In-store radio	• Telephone
• Books on tape/CD	• Kiosks	• Television
• CD ROMs	• Movies	• Toys
• Cartoons	• Multimedia	• Training programs
• DVDs	• Museums	• Websites
• Email	• Points of purchase	

Early Applications

Intercept Messages

The most widely recognized use of prerecorded voices on the telephone network are intercept messages. We've all heard these messages after dialing a number incorrectly. "The number you've dialed has been disconnected," or "All circuits are busy, please try your call again later." These messages communicate some sort of status to the caller.

Time and Temperature

Time and temperature systems were among the first widely used automated voice systems.

Answering Machines

The first commercially successful phone answering machine, PhoneMate, was introduced in the early 1970s. It was seen as a great technological advancement by some and as a rude awakening by others. "I just don't like talking to a machine" was uttered by many who were uncomfortable with the systems. Others spent hours creating off-the-wall outgoing messages. Fortunately, the communications advantages were recognized as a real plus in time management.

As the prices dropped later in the decade, it became a must-have for people on the go. Remember, this was long before the ease of inexpensive cellular phones made everyone instantly available. In the early 80s, anyone could afford a PhoneMate, Panasonic or Code-A-Phone answering machine.

In fact, the first commercial effort I made in producing audio for telephones was in creative outgoing messages for answering machines. I produced about a dozen off-the-shelf versions and ran ads in the local weekly paper, *Creative Loafing*. Here's one of the ads I ran in 1983:

These goofy messages were intended for use in people's home answering machines. Here's the script of one:

Sound Effects: Baseball Game

Announcer: *Thank you for calling, Ladies and Gentlemen, just as the person you're calling is stepping up to the plate. Here's the pitch ... it's a curve ball (slap) ... it's a drive to right field. He's heading to second for a double. Here's the throw ... he's, he's OUT. So leave a message after the tone.*

These efforts were not met with resounding success. In fact, I recall selling about a dozen messages.

When people think of answering machines, they usually think in terms of home usage. In the early 1980s, however, answering machines were handling phone calls after-hours for many businesses. Remember, this was before voice mail.

A cottage industry bubbled up to write creative messages for these machines. It was the everyday person's chance to be a star. You've heard some of those incredibly bad, silly or stupid messages. Then, as now, many outgoing messages were recorded by children. A Google search of answering machine messages returns over 400,000 listings.

Answering machines became a cultural platform for everyone to express their creativity via their outgoing message. Allyson Krieger did a great job describing the power that the answering machine played in our lives in this article that appeared on *WildWeb* on May 6, 1999.

THE MEDIUM IS THE MESSAGE
THE ANSWERING MACHINE AS POP CULTURE ORACLE
by Allyson Krieger
Reproduced with permission.

"Leave your name and number after the beep." Its words are a societal mantra, a phrase reworded and reworked into endless variations and emblazoned on our collective memory like a magical incantation. We come home after work, school or play, and it benignly sits there, looking deceptively innocent while holding all of our hopes, our dreams, our answers. Did I get the job? Will he really call? Are my test results back? It all lies within the flick of a button on the answering machine, our modern-day pop culture oracle.

The Golden Years

In college, my roommate and I had an old-fashioned Panasonic, the kind with a regular cassette you could play right on the stereo. We would never erase our messages, but instead we saved them like precious reminders of past friendships, parties and conquests. We'd have tapes upon tapes full of drunken babbling, giggling friends and, unfortunately, the occasional intrusive voice of the outside world disguised as parental concern. We kept them like oral diaries of our typical college lives—little black trophies to remind ourselves that we were popular, fun and funny. We played them when we were bored, or just to recall a voice or a moment.

Even the outgoing message we left for the public was a matter of national concern. Should we be flip or sexy? Sound busy? Laugh? Maybe we should play music in the background. Is a dance beat too cheesy? A ballad too sappy? A song slightly out of the mainstream was usually deemed best. It had to be something not too popular, but recognizable enough so people would understand that we were, in fact, cool.

Recording the agreed-upon message was a bonding session. We'd lock the door, hunker down around the magic machine, and practice a few times before making a go at it. Deep breath, cleared throat and, unavoidably, uncontrollable fits of laughter. Guaranteed. The more times it took to get it right, the more we laughed. By the time we nailed it, it was a validating moment equal to the satisfaction of 50 aced exams.

Then came the testing phase, as the new message got critiqued by friends calling one by one, telling us it was better than the old one or that we sounded weird, or asking who the guy was in the background. Sometimes our parents would hesitate for a moment, shocked at the sound of our new voices. "Um...hello? Is that you?" they would begin tenuously.

But nothing was more exhilarating than the moment we'd storm the room after a party, frat house or bar we'd snuck into, running breathlessly over to our little gray-and-black box. If the light was blinking: success. The more blinks, the better. Greedily, the roommate with the quicker trigger finger would begin the cycle with a reassuring whir of rewinding tape. What came next could make or break us—from a late-night call from the paramour down the hall to a friend in need of one last cigarette.

We'd be quiet, sometimes taking our coats off, but more often than not standing still in honor of the ritual. Sometimes we'd analyze a message with more precision than a team of scientists, looking for hidden meaning or words between the lines. If something was particularly good, we'd hit replay, wanting to savor the feeling of excitement or relief.

Current Era

Once we graduated from college, our answering machine habits matured right along with us. Outgoing messages need to be adult, tame and professional. We practice, this time sounding confident—we are adults now, after all, in control of our lives and proud of our newfound independence. And dammit, our words will reflect that. What if a prospective employer should call, or my boyfriend's mother?

Incoming messages too have changed in tone and nature. Doctors' appointments and workplace concerns replace party directions and 2 AM check-ins.

These days, digital answering machines and corporate voice mail have lessened the tangible rewards of old-time message retrieval. I no longer ferret tapes away like tiny oral histories, but treat my modern-day oracle like another piece of electronic equipment. Still, I respect its place in my life. New features, abilities and quality improvements have imbued the answering machine with even greater powers. Now it can tell me a phone number, replay instantaneously or stop on a dime. I can get my messages from work or a friend's house, making my machine a part of me wherever I am.

Remote message retrieval keeps us connected to our home and our jobs even when we're out of town, on the road or light years away. We know that the machine is there, no matter what, storing our lives for us when we're gone, in patient anticipation of our return. If we're awaiting an important call, we anxiously press the access code again and again into our cellular keypads, hoping each time for the rush of success.

Another new dimension that's entered our relationship with the answering machine is screening: the power the answering machine gives us over others to deem a caller's worth. Our time is carefully measured now, as must be our phone conversations. We let the machine act as our buffer against reality—if we don't want to deal, we don't pick up. Thank you, answering machine, for handling that one.

Want Proof? Pop Culture Evidence

Like any other piece of pop culture, the older generation doesn't really get answering machines. Grandparents who own one most likely received it as a gift from a well-intentioned son or daughter. Answering machines scare our elders—you can hear it in the messages they leave. Like PCs or pagers, they're electronic gadgets that, past a certain age, just don't resonate.

Further proof of the answering machine's cultural significance can be found in its place on television. A recent "Friends" episode revolved around a message left to Ross by his ex-wife Emily. Rachel inadvertently erased the message, leading to a prolonged ethical crisis of to tell or not to tell. The answering machine, foiled! Does Rachel intercept the words before they reach their intended recipient, or does she step aside the mission of relayed information?

"Friends" has used the theme before, in an especially funny episode that called into question the age of an answering machine message. The joke hinged on whether or not the message from Monica's former flame, Richard, was pre- or post-breakup. If it was new, hope! If it was old, what a tease. Again, the machine determines her fate.

The second "Friends" scenario mirrors our fear that the answering machine might fail us. God forbid a power outage or technical difficulties! We need to feel confident that our machines are performing their task with 100% efficiency. The power they have in our lives is absolute; we're totally reliant, at the whim of the tape.

And what better show for our little friend to cameo on than TV's pop culture king, "Seinfeld"? The answering machine has figured into no less than six episodes of the classic sitcom, joining the ranks of other modern situation gags like waiting in line, countertop tip jars, finding your car in a mall lot, and various types of "talkers." Once, George spars with the machine by leaving progressively nastier messages for a girlfriend; once, the message Jerry leaves a rival comedian ends up in her show; once, the "it's me" message is dissected by Jerry, et al.

Rewind

In Douglas Coupland's cyberculture treatise "Microserfs," he lists a handful of devices that have made their way into our entertainment arsenals. VCRs, cell phones, CDs and, of course, answering machines. The birth of these symbolic items permanently changed how we judge ourselves and others, introducing the concept of "having a life" and, conversely, not having one. For the answering machine's part, we're judged by our voice and our tone, how we build our relationship with our machine, and the way we incorporate it into our lives.

Coupland's argument places the answering machine as one piece of a whole, a set of innovations that have forever changed the state of pop culture. He's right, but for me, it's more than that. The answering machine has a unique place in modern times, both as part of a sweeping technological trend and as a distinct measure of self. The messages we leave and retrieve mirror the place we are in life, our social status, our friendships and romantic entanglements.

We entrust intimate secrets to others' machines and rely on ours to provide answers. Our outgoing greeting tells people more about us than we might realize. Both a day-to-day constant and a reflection of the big picture, it's all there, in that prophetic little box: our very own machine of dreams.

What do you think? What does your answering machine say about you? Do you have a funny answering machine story?

While answering machines were functioning as social quarterbacks for people like Allyson and others, it slowly became a tool used in business. Often companies with two to ten business lines would use a Code-A-Phone, Panasonic or other brand answering machine after hours. The machines would only answer one line at a time, however, which was a bit of a problem. If several calls came in at or near the same time, only the first line or call would be answered.

The solution was to buy two or three answering machines for the first lines in the rotary group. If the first line was busy, the second call would roll over to the next line and so on. I saw a number of large companies doing this in the early 1980s. It worked reasonably well by the standards of that day. It would, however, be a bit short by today's technological frame of reference. Here's the entertaining viewpoint of Ryan Eanes in an article he wrote after finding a Code-A-Phone in the basement office.

IT CRAWLED FROM THE BINS: THE CODE-A-PHONE
by Ryan Eanes
Reproduced with Permission

Although this is a product that was manufactured probably in the late 1970s, we didn't know of its existence until recently when we were cleaning out the junky basement area at the Upper Room. Apparently this thing is the first answering machine ever created, and it was, for whatever reason, named the Code-A-Phone. Let's consider this title for a moment.

1) Nothing is actually being "coded" anywhere, since it probably operates using reel-to-reel tape that can't be replaced...at least not in a readily apparent manner.

2) How does one "code a phone" exactly? This device doesn't provide an adequate answer.

3) Thankfully the Code-A-Phone Corporation has ceased to operate. Either that or it was acquired by someone else in a merger. And I'm sure that that business (probably Atari) has ceased operation as well.

Now for a frightening image of this device:

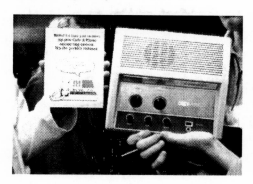

Note that it is basically knob-operated and has three buttons labeled "Rewind," "Play" and "Record." The leftmost knob is some sort of volume control that has since ceased to operate, and the rightmost knob is labeled from left to right "Off," "Record," "Play," "Listen" and "Answer." According to the manual, this is supposed to be user-intuitive. Now, I am a college-educated person, and I had difficulty figuring this one out. Unlike the ballots in Florida, this thing really IS baffling.

1) How is "Play" different from "Listen"?

21) Why are there both a "Record" function setting and a "Record" button? Are they independent functions, or do you have to use one to use the other?

3) How do you "Stop"? There is no such button. Do you unplug it? Do you turn the knob to "Off"? Do you hit it repeatedly until it stops doing whatever?

4) Why would one want to use the "Record" button while having the knob turned to "Off," "Play," "Listen" or "Answer"? There are almost an infinite number of questions we could ask like this based on the number of knob settings there are.

5) And most importantly, how are you supposed to "Erase" anything? Or is this like a Kodak one-use camera in that you use it until all the tape is gone and then throw it away and buy a new one? That seems like a big waste.

Also note the small window and little indicator light located directly above my left hand in the photo. This is the thing that tells you how many messages you have. Not NEW messages, mind you, but messages overall. So I assume that once the light is on, it's on for good, considering the machine's inability to erase. This window is not an LCD or LED display like most modern answering machines feature; nay nay, this is instead a small black plastic disk with numbers from 0 to (I would guess) 15 that rotates beneath the window as messages accumulate. I don't know what it does once it exceeds the number that the disk can show...perhaps it displays something like >15.

We were able to revive the Code-A-Phone long enough to play the messages that it was holding (the little window said "2" when we found it.) The first was a redneck woman with a hideous Southern accent saying, "Testing the Code-A-Phone. Testing the Code-A-Phone. Testing the Code-A-Phone to see if it works. [Pause] Hello. Testing the Code-A-Phone. Testing the Code-A-Phone. Hello. [Longer pause] Testing the Code-A-Phone to see if it works." Apparently after they "tested" this device (in multiple ways), it was found to be unsatisfactory and sat in our junkroom for the 32 years since.

Probably the most alarming aspect of this whole deal is the presence of the "postcards" that William is holding. They read (in case you can't see it clearly in the photo):

Hello! I'd like you to meet my new Code-A-Phone Answering System. It's the perfect listener.

[inside a voice bubble] *And I promise that I'll never talk back.* [Beep.]

The front cover of the package for these cards read (this emphasis was there already), "You may notice that some people are apprehensive about talking to a machine. This is a syndrome called hang-up syndrome. Fortunately, this is a simple thing to overcome! Simply take a 'humorous greeting card' from this book, fill in an address, write a personal message, and mail! It's that easy to introduce your friends to your new Code-A-Phone Answering System!"

I don't think I have to say a word about the stupidity of mailing postcards to your friends about your answering machine. Apparently the Code-A-Phone Corporation was at least slightly aware of this, as there were only eight postcards included. Only people with eight friends (or fewer) would bother to MAIL these ridiculous and nonfunny cards to their friends...and if they did, that would be eight fewer people who would ever take you seriously again.

Digital Announcers

In the early 1980s, the digital announcer started to make a difference, replacing many of the answering machines in phone rooms across the country. These units were manufactured by companies like Interalia and Cook. They could stand alone or interface with larger PBXs, switches and Automatic Call Distributors (ACDs) in customer service operations. That was before they were referred to as call centers.

As with all new technology, their features and capabilities grew over the years. The first units were designed to have a customer service agent read the delay and after-hours messages into a handset in the phone room or on the receptionist's console. The quality of these recording was usually not very good. From a performance standpoint, it was a throw of the dice as to how good it would sound. The technical aspects were almost always bad because of the equipment noise, the office chatter and the cheesy handset or mic that was supplied.

When we were called in to upgrade the quality on the recordings, it was difficult to get our professionally recorded messages into these units. We had to create a variety of couplers to take the output from a cassette tape deck and feed it into a handset coupler or modular phone cord jack. It was trial and error, but once we learned how to load the studio-produced messages into a particular brand or model, it was simple. We'd document the process and move on to the next one.

On-Hold Programs

Well into the 1990s, the radio was the most often used source for on-hold background music. The people running the telecommunications departments just didn't think about what was being played to their callers while they were waiting for an agent: everything from horrible news stories and obnoxious music to fast-talking DJs and competitors' advertisements.

Who was in charge of the radio, what station they chose and how loud it was could vary greatly. If Mildred in Accounting was calling the shots, it would be a nice easy-listening station. But if Wanda in Sales wanted to boogie, she'd put it on 96Rock or something else loud and proud. What did that say to the customer who was placed on hold for three minutes? Companies were lucky if their music even remotely matched the image they were trying to project.

The idea to run prerecorded messages while callers were on hold was rather novel at the time. When people first started hearing them, they thought it was pretty cool, but the novelty wore off as they continued to hold. Still, it was a great medium: The caller was interested enough to call, and you promoted the benefits of other items while they waited.

I had a personal conflict with the approach many of the on-hold message companies were taking then, which seemed to boil down to, "They're a captured audience, sell them more." My position was more like, "Help the time pass more quickly by sharing information of value." In hindsight, they were basically the same tactics, different deliveries. Today's equivalent may be spam: One man's helpful information is another man's spam.

Music Licensing Fees

An even larger problem was looming about that time: music licensing fees. Did you know that every time you hear a song played on the radio, the person who wrote that song collects a few pennies?

Just think about that for a minute. Let's say you get an inspiration one evening while thinking about how much you love your spouse. You take pen to paper and write a terrific love song. You mail it off to Sheryl Crow, who falls in love with it and puts it on her next album. Did you know that every time that song is played on a radio station, on a television show or at an event, a usage fee is paid to the composer?

The fees aren't paid directly to the composer for practical reasons. To solve this payment-collection dilemma, two organizations act on behalf of all those songwriters out there. The American Society of Composers, Authors and Publishers (ASCAP) and Broadcast Music, Inc. (BMI) manage this process for the writers.

Now back to your song. Let's say your song goes to number one on the *Billboard* charts and is played by thousands of stations and networks every day for years. Everybody loves it and soon the royalty checks start rolling in. Hey, you're set for life! Well, unless you practiced your music and songwriting for two hours a day as a kid, are very talented, and are luckier than the latest lottery winner, that's probably not in the cards.

How do these music licensing fees affect music-on-hold? When you plug the radio into your telephone system, you are rebroadcasting those songs on your phone system. You become one of the outlets that must pay a usage fee to the music licensing groups who'll then pay the songwriter. In the eyes of the law, if a company is not paying these fees, it is stealing.

Here's what ASCAP and BMI have to say about it today on their websites:

AMERICAN SOCIETY OF COMPOSERS, AUTHORS AND PUBLISHERS
from <u>www.ascap.com</u>

Q) *I want to use music-on-hold in my business. Do I need permission?*

A) Yes. When you place a caller on hold and transmit music via your telephone lines, that is a public performance of the music. It is your responsibility to obtain permission to perform ASCAP songs from ASCAP or directly from the copyright owner. ASCAP represents tens of thousands of copyright owners and millions of songs, and an ASCAP license will give you the right to perform them all.

BROADCAST MUSIC, INC.
From <u>www.bmi.com</u>

Music-On-Hold

When your business uses music-on-hold, you must first obtain permission from the copyright owners for the use of that music in your business. To accomplish this, you would have to determine who the songwriters and publishers are for each song you want to use and then negotiate a fee with each of them in order for you to play their copyrighted music legally. BMI offers you a much easier solution: a Music Performance Agreement. With it, you pay a reasonable annual fee, which authorizes you to use approximately 4.5 million copyrighted musical works by over 300,000 of the world's leading songwriters, composers and music publishers who are affiliated with BMI.

To many people, this licensing issue seemed more of a sales technique for the handful of ASCAP and BMI salespeople around the country, helping them close a lot of deals over the years. You may notice that many restaurants have a little sticker on the front door that states, "Member of ASCAP" or "Member of BMI." The sticker is to reassure customers that they have paid the proper royalties for their background music in the lobby and on the telephone.

The licensing rules also helped GM Voices close more messages-on-hold program sales, which were a large part of our business at the time. Our agreements with our music library providers stipulated that our clients would not be required to pay any fees directly to ASCAP or BMI. In effect, the usage fees we paid to the library providers covered use on telephone systems. We also used some music libraries whose composers were not members of ASCAP or BMI, eliminating the need for those fees.

Message-On-Hold Companies

Later on, a number of companies around the country, including GM Voices, started writing and producing six-minute on-hold audio programs that allowed callers to hear information about the company's products and services. The messages psychologically reduced the time spent on hold because the caller's attention was focused more on the information and less on the time spent holding. It was a great solution.

As long at the hold time was brief, it was a good venue to share information about new products and services, operational issues, and even community involvement. It was basically just another channel to use in communicating with customers.

Some clients would express concern that customers were getting irritated by the messages. When we drilled down on the problem, it turned out the callers were on hold for 10 to 15 minutes. That means they heard the entire program, with its snappy little messages, two or three times. How many times can you hear "Your call is important to us" and "The next available representative will be right with you" and not get annoyed? That problem needs to be corrected by hiring more people to answer the phone.

Message-On-Hold Formats

The loop tapes came in 1, 3, 6 and 12-minute versions. Most of our on-hold programs were 6 minutes, with music throughout, and contained about 8 messages of 15-20 seconds each.

Here's what a typical 6-minute program looked like:

Messages	#1	#2	#3	#4	#5	#6	#7	#8
Time								

───→

| Minutes :00 | | 1:00 | 2:00 | 3:00 | 4:00 | 5:00 | 6:00 | |

Sample On-Hold Program Script

The scripts were usually simple and each message focused on one idea. Here's a sample of an on-hold script:

#1 Business Hours

Male: Thank you for calling WidgetCo. We appreciate your call. At WidgetCo, customer satisfaction is our primary concern. That's why we have a professional staff ready to help you with any questions or comments. For your convenience, our office hours are weekdays from 9 AM to 6 PM Eastern Time. Thank you for holding, we'll be right with you.

#2 Our Philosophy

Female: What makes WidgetCo different? Quality products and dependability. We are committed to your total satisfaction. We have a professional staff dedicated to assisting you five days a week, Monday through Friday, from 9 AM to 6 PM Eastern Standard Time. At WidgetCo, we do whatever it takes to make you happy. Put your trust in WidgetCo!

3 Staff Training

Male: Did you know that all of our installers are professionally trained and certified through the International Widget

Association? That means you can expect the finest workmanship in the industry. And since we are a local company, we're always there when you need us! At WidgetCo, we are dedicated to excellence!

4 Products

Female: With the cost of office space escalating, it is important for you to get the most out of what you have. With WidgetCo's lateral filing system, you can save more than half your existing filing space. A Mobile Storage System eliminates aisle space and saves up to 75% in floor space over conventional drawer files. Ask your WidgetCo sales representative for a free space analysis.

#5 Surveys

Male: Every year, we at WidgetCo like to get a better feel for our customers' satisfaction level. We are taking a new approach this year by offering the convenience of customer surveys online! To take the online survey, go to W W W dot WidgetCo dot com. Just look for the survey button. Your opinion and feedback is VERY important to us. We appreciate your helping us to serve your needs more efficiently.

#6 Trade Shows

Female: Meat and poultry processors, WidgetCo will be at the Worldwide Food Expo, October 28th through 31st. Come see us in Booth 5307 in the Meat, Poultry and Seafood Hall. See WidgetCo's latest food-processing belts, designed to reduce your costs and raise your profits. For more details about the Worldwide Food Expo, or more information on WidgetCo food-processing belts for your application, contact our marketing department at Extension 3246.

#7 Customers Talk

Male: More WidgetCo customers are speaking up about how our solutions make their live easier. Here's what Jack Tarson of Fremont, California, has to say. "When we first installed the system, we were confident it was a good decision. After it was up and running for three months, it was clearly a great decision. We reduced our costs about 35%. We'll add another system next quarter."

#8 Staff Anniversary

Female: Next time you talk to Mandy Jackson, please congratulate her for her recent anniversary here at WidgetCo. She just completed her seven year anniversary with WidgetCo. Thanks for the great effort, Mandy!

Markets

Producing on-hold programs became a large part of our business. At one point in the early 90s, they represented over 90% of our revenue. One of the markets GM Voices pioneered was the cable television industry. As you may recall, being placed on hold when calling your cable company was an almost certainty in the 80s and 90s. The wait times were often very long. At one point, we provided on-hold programs to nearly 300 different cable companies around the country.

The unique nature of the cable business was great for us. The on-hold messages were largely focused on cable channels like HBO, Showtime, Arts & Entertainment. The networks changed their programs every month, which meant the cable company needed a new tape every month!

Playback Equipment

There were only a few playback options. From 1984 to 1990, the majority of message-on-hold programs were delivered on loop tapes. The digital announcer manufacturers were still focused on ACD and after-hours messaging, and were just starting to create announcers for on-hold-message playback. Loop tapes were cheap, they'd play nonstop for months, and you only needed a desktop tape deck for playback.

A few message-on-hold providers used auto-reverse tape decks, but they didn't seem to stand the test of time. We purchased thousands of the Panasonic Trimline desktop tape decks for about $20 each. There may still be some out there playing. If one broke, we just threw it away and plugged in another one. We could have used more expensive tape decks, but price made little difference in playback sound, quality or longevity.

The digital announcer manufacturers soon started altering their equipment to work with on-hold applications. There's no question that storing the audio recording on a computer chip was more dependable than the loop tapes. Like any electronic device, they were expensive initially, but came down in a few years. The digital announcers really began to move when cassette tape drives were built in to automatically load the program when a new tape was inserted. Today, of course, it's all done remotely.

Call Sequencers and ACDs

Call sequencers and automatic call distributors allowed companies to manage the flow of calls into their operations more effectively because call volumes at most businesses follow predictable patterns. During high-volume spikes, these devices acted like traffic cops to direct the flow. During those times when staffing resources were taxed, the devices would answer the calls and play delay messages such as:

All our agents are busy now. Please hold and the next available representative will be with you shortly."

Then the caller heard the radio or an on-hold-message program. Again, in the early days, an on-staff customer service agent recorded the message. In 1985, GM Voices began to help companies with the scripting of their applications. One of our first large implementations using this technology was Delta Air Lines.

At the time, Delta had 17 reservations centers around the country. The message you heard depended on where you were calling from, because a reservations agent in each call center recorded that center's messages. So some of the messages were OK, but quite a few did not present Delta with the image people expected.

One of their problems was the script. Here are the words that were spoken before we helped them:

Thank you for calling Delta Air Lines. All agents are busy now.
Please wait and the next available agent will be with you as soon as possible."

Conceptually, it doesn't make sense to tell someone who's called to book a flight that you're too busy to answer their call. And it just wasn't good manners for a Southern company. We changed the script subtlely to:

We appreciate your calling Delta Air Lines.
All our agents are currently assisting other callers. Please wait and the next available agent will be right with you.

Voice Mail

Gordon Mathews patented his Voice Message Express in 1982. He started his company, VMX, in Dallas in 1979. His first system was sold to 3M and, as was often the case with startups, his wife recorded the prompts and greetings on the first commercial voice mail system. Over the ensuing years, a number of successful companies grew voice mail into the ubiquitous medium it became. VMX was purchased by Octel, which was purchased by Lucent, which spun it off as Avaya. Rolm/Siemens and Nortel completed the circle of large voice mail players. An army of smaller systems emerged when Dialogic, founded in 1983 and purchased by Intel in 1999, created boards that allowed developers to create lower-cost, PC-based voice mail systems.

Voice mail became a very powerful tool. While there was an initial backlash as some people were offended when their calls weren't answered by a "human being," the technology was soon seen as a great productivity boost. The phrase "telephone tag" was coined as people left messages over and over for each other, thinking they needed to talk real time.

Luckily, the voice mail manufacturers and voice mail enthusiasts encouraged callers to "leave detailed messages" so they could act on the information. As callers used voice mail in "time-shifting," voice mail began to reach its potential. No longer did we have to speak to other people to complete our transactions.

Another popular time-shifting vehicle is the VCR. Assuming you can figure out how to work it, you can record a television show and watch it later. We essentially shifted time from a moment that was convenient for the caller or the television network to a time convenient for us.

Time-shifting is an important process to master if you want to be productive today. Email is another version of this technique. (I'm not sure where instant messaging fits into the program; it almost seems like going backward.)

Automated Attendant

The automated attendant is a great application that's gotten a bad rap over the years. I can't tell you how many times I've heard, "I want to talk to a real person so I always just press 0." Well, sometimes I do it, too. I have a particular interest in the automated attendant, however, because we write the scripts and produce the voices for thousands of these systems every year. Many of the ones we fix are the poorly designed ones GM Voices staff members happen to reach as consumers.

"Boy, you need to call this one," a staff member will say. They'll dial it up on the conference room phone, and groans are heard all around. Not only do many auto attendants sound bad, but the call flows and scripts often have no logic to them.

Ha! But isn't that true with lots of cutting-edge technologies? At first glance, manufacturers see how many problems the new product will solve, and there's a mad rush to get it out to the marketplace and make a million dollars. Only in the rush to be the leader, a few issues are not fully considered, such as user interface, the end user, installation support, etc.

Get Rid of the Receptionist

In the 1980s, when automated attendant systems first began to appear, there was a great deal of enthusiasm from the accounting department. Here was the pitch from the person selling the system:

Sales:	*Now, how much are you paying your receptionist?*
Customer:	*I think she makes about $18,000. Why do you ask?*
Sales:	*Well, Mr. Prospect, this is your lucky day. You can give her the pink slip today. The new Super Duper Acme Automated Attendant will start answering your calls tomorrow. No salary, no benefits, no calling in sick, and it works 24 hours a day, 365 days a year.*
Customer:	*It'll really do all that?*
Sales:	*That and more. It also will . . .*

So across the country, slick-talking salespeople sold systems left and right as a way to cut the receptionist expense. Thousands of systems were installed without much thought given to call flows, scripts or zero-out options. At first, it was novel and interesting. "Hey, you've got to call into this number and listen to it" was uttered many times. But the novelty wore off when callers couldn't get to the person they were calling. They often couldn't get to any real person.

So a swell of anti-automated attendant and anti-voice mail sentiment bubbled up and gave the technology a bit of a black eye. People viewed it as a way for companies to save money by eliminating staff without any real consideration given to the customers who wanted to buy something.

Over time, the companies selling the technology got better and society as a whole began to warm up to this new customer self-service technology.

Today, most companies use automated attendants and customers are OK with it, as long as they can accomplish their objective with reasonable efficiency. With the addition of well-designed speech recognition capability, it truly is a better caller experience.

Interactive Voice Response (IVR)

One of the most successful computer telephony applications is the IVR. It marries telephone voice automation to a database. With this union, people can get most any type of information they need by phone. The banking, brokerage and financial industries were the first beneficiaries. Just imagine the cost savings when IVRs freed bank employees from researching routine requests about cleared checks, transfers and account balances. It was as huge productivity gain. Functionality has continued to improve and now speech recognition technology is taking IVR systems to entire new levels of capability.

Speech Recognition

Speech recognition can be employed in lots of applications. This user-interface technique allows users to speak their commands into the phone instead of pressing touchtone buttons.

Speech recognition has dramatically raised the level of quality required and expected in prerecorded voices for telecommunications applications. The more naturally the caller speaks, the greater the chance the system will accurately recognize the caller's utterance. So the objective in producing greetings and voice prompts for speech is to sound natural so the caller will reply naturally.

When IVR developers first realized they needed to use professional voices for their applications, they recruited big-voice radio announcers. These disk jockeys and reporter types from radio had nice voices and they pronounced words accurately, but they didn't sound like real people. They were almost caricatures. They spoke in an unnatural cadence and pronounced each word as a separate entity. By repeating this process over and over, they made a sentence. You can understand them, but it doesn't sound real.

The voice actors we've always used at GM Voices are theatrically trained and know how to perform scripts like a real person. That's why we're the leading independent provider of voices to the speech-recognition industry.

Who's Answering the Phone?

All the automated voice applications we've discussed so far use prerecorded voices to answer the phone, route callers, provide information and conduct transactions. But whose voice is heard on these systems? And how do the applications impact which voices are chosen?

Let's look at a typical phone system installation and how the voice might be recruited. Then we'll look at how the particular applications drive the choice of voices.

Typical Phone System Install

A typical phone system installation involves many challenges and difficulties. No matter what applications are included in the "cut-over," the last thing anyone's concerned about is the prerecorded voices that'll be needed on the system.

Installing a phone system is usually a big deal for a company regardless of its size. With few exceptions, the telephone is the critical link to prospects and customers. When the phone system goes down, sales often come to an immediate halt. Keeping the lines of communication open with your prospects and customers is critical. So let's say that a new phone system is being installed at SlamCo so they can communicate more effectively with their customers. The system has lots of cool new features that will help them sell more and increase their leadership role in the slammer space.

The project manager for the system provider is Richard Blake. He oversees dozens of these cut-overs every year. He's been through the drill. He's seasoned and confident. He knows that some ugly problem will raise its head during the installation, but he has the tools and experience to deal with it calmly. All the preliminary work has been completed, all the orders with the dial-tone provider relating to configuration changes were placed, and his team will be ready when the magic moment comes to pull the plug on the old system tonight.

Everything goes smoothly for the first two hours, but when they try to go live, there's some problem at the local phone company's central office. Turns out that the order to the dial-tone guys was not completed correctly. In addition, the power supply for the new system is dead on arrival. Then Richard's chief installer is called away on a family emergency—his daughter broke her arm at a gymnastics meet.

So it's "battle stations." The normal problems expected at a cut-over are multiplied by about four and his chief lieutenant is missing in action. "This is going to be a little too exciting," Richard thinks. The pressure is on. He's got to get the system up and running by 9 AM the next morning or face the considerable wrath of the SlamCo's operations manager.

Fast forward. It's 7 AM and everyone is tired. Richard and his team went through Herculean efforts to get SlamCo's system up and running, including tracking down the dial-tone guys at midnight, digging up a refurbished power supply from a competitor, and clearing a few other hurdles too complicated to mention. All the challenges were met with a collective eye on victory—a working system by 9 AM. While the ops manager will nod his head in appreciation when he hears about the heroic efforts, he won't really understand and probably won't care.

The system is working, so now they need to record the automated attendant greetings and menus. The conversation goes something like this:

Richard: *OK, we need to get someone to record the messages on the system. Who do you want to do that?*

Ops Mgr: *I don't know. Can't you do it?*

Richard: *I can have one of my guys do it. Don't you want to record it? You're the operations manager.*

Ops Mgr: *I'm not going to do it. I don't want to talk to any more customers than I have to.*

Richard: *How about the receptionist? Is she here yet?*

Ops Mgr: *Yeah, Cindy. I saw her a minute ago.*

Richard: *OK. So, it's either Cindy the receptionist or Bob the installer. Who will it be?*

Chosen voices fall into two broad categories: in-house and outsourced. As is true with any attempt to categorize a group of activities or performances, there is gray area between the groups. Keep in mind, too, that this is a discussion of the voices only and how they might be cast in this role. The broader solution options are discussed in the sections on Persona and Voice Branding Specialist.

In-House Voices

The vital part of the story with in-house solutions is that the person who "owns" the brand is not in the loop. The phone is a critical link with customers and prospects—too critical to leave to the phone people.

With in-house voice solutions, some large companies have held auditions to pick an employee to be the voice of the company. These solutions were more widespread in years past, but as the technology became more sophisticated, they've gotten more difficult to administer.

People often ask whether callers prefer a male or female. In the 20+ years I've been in this field, I've noticed that most companies choose a female for their prerecorded voices. I think it's because executives have historically expected the person answering the phone to be a woman, and putting a female voice on the system was just the continuation of that thinking. It is changing now; speech recognition systems are using male voices much more frequently.

With the adoption of more speech recognition technology, the bar is being rapidly raised to achieve quality more along the lines that companies exhibit in other areas of their business. It only makes sense when you consider their ongoing brand building.

We have three voice choices—Bob, Cindy or Todd. While Bob actually works for the phone provider, the level of naturalness and quality he delivers is consistent with that of Cindy the receptionist and Todd the marketing manager. It's a crap shoot as to how the end result will work and sound.

The Installer: Bob

Bob gets roped into becoming the voice for SlamCo simply because he knows the sequence. He writes out a script he thinks makes sense and shows it to the ops manager, who grunts his approval. With all the noise of an office waking up, Bob records the messages and goes back to cleaning up the installation mess.

The Receptionist: Cindy

The scenario with Cindy is much the same. She is chosen because she is nearby when they need the greetings and menus recorded and because she's been answering the company phone for years. Management figures that the automated attendant system will be less jarring for callers this way because they'll be hearing the same voice they've always heard. This seems to make sense. Cindy's very excited about being the voice of the company.

The Customer Service Manager: Todd

Todd is the guy everybody thinks about when they need a voice. He's got a very deep, nice-sounding voice. He actually sings with a barber shop quartet, so it's right up his alley.

Here are a few points you need to consider about in-house solutions:

What if the employee quits?

When the employee leaves the company, a sudden vacuum appears. In a number of examples I recall, the president's wife was the voice talent. It was great until divorce proceedings began.

Is it actually cheaper?

When you look at the fully loaded cost of employees administering, recording and managing this process, the savings are lost in a poorly applied resource. With the competitive nature of business today, it's all about core competencies. This is a core competency for only a handful of companies in the US.

What will the technical sound quality be?

The technical aspects of recording quality messages are tough, because Cindy's only using a $25 handset on the phone system, which make it hard to compete with a high-fidelity studio setup.

What will the performance sound quality be?

There is some surprisingly good employee voice talent in the marketplace. One of the core voice actors in the GM Voices stable got her start as an employee voice talent. The majority, however, are unable to perform as well as professional voice actors. On larger applications with hundreds of prompts, the production chain of quality usually falls apart.

Will the person be available regularly?

Sometimes the employee is in demand in other areas of the business, making timely changes and updates to messages problematic. It becomes a tug of war between those department supervisors.

Is the company studio set up for this type of recording?

Some larger companies have their own sophisticated recording studios. You'd think this would be a win-win for everybody, but I've seen this work effectively only a few times over the years. Even then, it may have been personal pride not to admit it wasn't a good solution. Corporate recording studios are usually used to produce training videos or sales-promotion programs for the troops in the field.

The production staff often thinks recording voices for the phone is beneath their expert station in life. They should really be producing movies, right? And the in-house engineers in the production department don't know anything about getting the finished recordings into the systems that will play them. And with multiple systems in use, it's all the more difficult to get them up and running.

The issue of availability is probably more pronounced here than with the staff member as the voice talent. Other "more important" projects invariably interrupt recording sessions or delivery.

OutSourced Voices

OutSourced voices are those from the professional arena. The definition gets a little slippery here, particularly between voice talent and voice actor. They can be the same, but they really aren't. While announcers call themselves voice talent and voice talent calls themselves voice actors, it is truly difficult to fit them into these categories. It's not that important anyway, because the end result is about the way they perform and you can't put that in a book. You can only put that in your ear!

For the sake of our discussion, I've noted my definitions below. They are based on 20+ years in the voiceover business in general and the computer telephony space in particular.

The Announcer: Rocky

Rocky works at the local radio station. He has a professional-sounding voice and great enunciation. He worked at his college radio station and made the jump to a commercial station six years ago. He has a big, deep voice, but he doesn't sound like that guy on the trailers at the movies. He speaks with that radio cadence we all hear when listening to our favorite stations. "That's Coldplay from their latest album, 'Parachutes.' I'll have the update on the weather right after this word from Taylor Automotive Group on Tallgrass Parkway." He's one of those who doesn't sound like a real person.

As part of his radio gig, he works a lot of on-site promotions at car dealers, shopping centers and clubs. He does the voiceover for a number of retailers in town that advertise on his station. He started recording the voice greeting for phone systems when one of his car dealer accounts asked him to voice their automated attendant. He doesn't get involved in the technical stuff. He just records the script in the studio and delivers it on cassette tape or records it into the phone system using the handset.

The Voice Talent: Emily

Emily can read a script with the emotion of the message. While a voice talent doesn't sound like a real person either, they sound like regular people *think* real people sound. I know that reeks of psychobabble, but here's the logic. To read conversationally, a voice talent has to be slightly more animated than a real person. They take the script and read it like a character would.

Some voice talent can make the transition to performing as voice actors, but even though announcers call themselves voice talent, they could never successfully perform as voice actors.

The Voice Actor: Sharon

Sharon studied drama in college and today earns her living using her voice in commercial, narration and creative productions. She can become the personality and portray the character identified in the biography provided with the script.

The difference between an announcer, a voice talent and a voice actor is difficult to articulate, but you know it when you hear it. The voice actor sounds more believable, more trustworthy, more like a friend sharing an experience with you. Like when you see a movie that makes you cry. You have been pulled into the story. You believe what you're seeing and hearing. You are immersed in the drama. When the emotions are on screen and you're feeling them as if you were part of the story, it's Hollywood, yes indeed.

Production Chain of Quality

Any of the mentioned solutions can work reasonably well when circumstances align so that each link in the production lineup for optimum performance. Imagine for a moment the entire process that's involved in getting these greetings, menus and voice prompts recorded. We call it the production chain. As with any sequence, its strength and quality is only as good as its weakest link.

Path of Least Resistance

What determines which voices are chosen? It depends on a number of factors and the path of least resistance. The type of voice offered in a solution will vary depending on the application, the developer, the integrator and the client's frame of reference. At cut-over time, the technical guys are all about getting the dial-tone turned on and starting the flow of calls. That's a good thing. The by-product is often

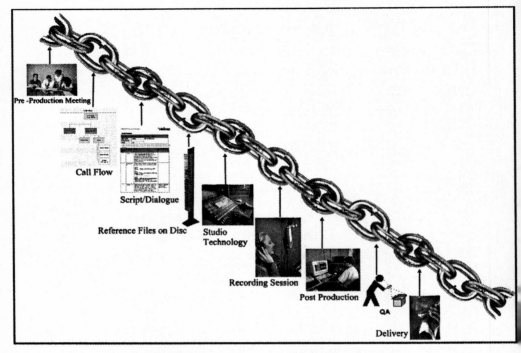

Pre-Production Meeting

Call Flow

Script/Dialogue

Reference Files on Disc

Studio Technology

Recording Session

Post Production

QA

Delivery

that they don't care about the "soft" issues, such as what voice is on the greetings, menus and system voice prompts.

Here's where the path of least resistance normally flows based on the technology:

Application	Voice
Automated Attendant	In-House
On-Hold Messages	Radio Announcer
ACD/Call Center Queues	In-House
IVR	Voice Talent
Speech Recognition	Voice Actors

Let's look at each of those components and examine how the voice choices stack up.

Automated Attendant

Most of the companies selling these systems in the past were very interested in selling systems, but not very concerned about how the system sounded once it was installed. As someone with a production and creative background, I think it really boils down to money. The sales reps have rarely been compensated for selling professional voices. Or if they were, it was such a small amount that it didn't get their attention.

Companies spend millions of dollars crafting their image in the marketplace, but after all this investment to convince the prospect to call, the automated call-handling process doesn't support their brand. It's the equivalent of allowing the offices out in the field to create their own brochures. It doesn't make sense.

So most of the touchtone-driven automated attendant systems in use today feature the voice of the receptionist or other staff member. Companies with a dozen (or a hundred) locations use a different voice at each location.

On-Hold Messages

Most on-hold systems today are "barge-in" systems: the six-minute audio program plays constantly on the digital announcer with an output being fed into the phone system. The program plays through once, then loops and plays again and again. When callers are placed on hold, they are dropped into this loop. That's why you often only hear the last part of a message. It's not ideal, but it works well for an inexpensive on-hold solution.

The price of entry to this space is very low. You only need a tape deck and a microphone to profess to be in the on-hold-message production business. It has become a real commodity in the market today. There are thousands of people working out of their basements who will record a new message for $15. As is true in most places, however, you generally get what you pay for. These programs almost always use announcer-grade voices who would be unable to perform as voice actors. Occasionally there will be a good result, but the planets must align for all the links in the production chain to perform flawlessly.

The providers in this space will often supply voices for automated attendant applications, but it's rarely an orchestrated effort.

ACD Messages

Years ago, the ACD providers, such as Rockwell and Aspect, didn't want to be troubled with prerecorded voice issues. They'd suggest that the client find a voice on their own. Again, it was not in the sales staff's compensation. As more technology providers are including ACD features in their offerings, some are now also offering voice production services.

Voice Mail

Most voice mail providers produced the system or generic voice prompts that come installed on their systems, and used professional voices to do so. It was, and still is, rare for those providers to make it easy for end users to obtain customized greetings, such as the company's name, in the same voices. When they do, the delivery times are longer and the costs are higher than solutions provided by voice branding specialists like GM Voices. Also, they typically have only one or two voices from which to choose.

IVR

Most of today's IVR providers either have in-house production resources or work with a professional studio for prerecorded voices on their applications. The quality of voice varies greatly.

Speech Recognition

Speech recognition technology providers, such as ScanSoft (SpeechWorks) and Nuance, have dramatically raised the quality of prerecorded voice in telecom applications. The voice actor is a pivotal player in speech recognition. His or her performance in a speech application sets the tone and feel. Luckily, the technology has become very accurate at recognizing the caller's requests and the voice actor provides a human comfort level that is not often associated with technology.

Over time, the quality and naturalness of the voices in speech recognition will find their way to the other customer-touching automated voices in the enterprise.

Persona

When people ask me what GM Voices does, I explain that we produce the prerecorded voices heard when you call the bank, drive a car with GPS, ride in a train, or prepare to board a plane at the airport. We record voice actors in our studios every day. I usually get a look of surprise and a reply like this:

Wow, I never thought about that. Guess someone has to do it.
Oh, aren't those computers or machines?
Yeah, I've heard those before. That's you guys?

Sometimes I forget how unique what we do is. The voiceover business used to be about recording for radio and television commercials and documentaries. Most other nonbroadcast uses were called "industrial." They were most often training or sales-promotion videos. The telecommunications space was a new frontier for voiceovers, starting with the delay messages you heard when your call was answered by a machine instead of a person. After a minute or two of music and/or messages, your call was connected to a real person.

As the technology evolved to include voice mail, automated attendant and IVR applications, the demand for prerecorded voices grew as well. These technologies came to the marketplace in a dizzying array of brands, configurations and features. And just like other electronics, they've gotten better and feature-rich over the years.

When speech recognition started to work its way out of the lab and into real commercial applications, the need for good voices again expanded. There was, however, an important difference with speech recognition. Where the radio announcer types, who were used by the majority of on-hold program providers, were OK for those other applications, they didn't work as well with speech recognition.

As the industry becomes more specialized in creating voice personalities for speech recognition applications and broader "voice branding initiatives," the solution options are becoming more robust. And more believable voices mean better speech applications.

What is a Persona?

Persona is more than a pithy resume and list of character traits. It is the "person" who talks with customers via this array of automated technology. Much like the personalities in a television drama or comedy, a persona is the friend you come to know and trust over time. The persona is the result of a team effort that includes a number of players:

- Voice actor
- Voice coach
- VUI designer
- Programmers
- Provider project manager
- Client project manager

The concept of persona has been promoted very effectively in the speech-recognition industry by the two leading technology providers: Nuance and ScanSoft (ScanSoft acquired SpeechWorks in 2003). Both of these companies recognized early on that the voice-user interface (VUI) was a critical link in creating successful speech applications. The persona is the leading part of the VUI because it is what actually touches the customer in a practical sense.

Although the word "persona" is most often used in the context of speech-recognition applications, it is much broader. The majority of automated voice technologies heard in the marketplace today are touchtone-driven. The caller is instructed to enter codes or account numbers using the touchtone key pad on the phone to access information or route their call. Whether touchtone or speech recognition, a persona answers the phone.

A company's persona, is evident throughout their enterprise's voice applications (automated attendant, IVR, call center queue, delay and after-hours messages). Corporate voice personalities outside the realm of speech implementations are just beginning to be noticed by branding-conscious organizations. While some executives will insist they do not have a persona at their company, they clearly do. It may be a hodge-podge of voices at different locations and departments across the country, but it is a persona. It's just not a very good one.

If you look to *Merriam-Webster* for a definition, you get:

Per·sona (*noun*)
> Etymology: Latin—more at **PERSON**
1): personae plural: the characters of a fictional presentation (as a novel or play) <comic personae>
2): plural personas \-n z\: the social front, facade, or mark an individual assumes to depict to the world at large. The role in life that he is playing—often contrasted with anima in the analytic psychology of C. G. Jung; compare **EGO**

In the book *Voice User Interface Design* by Michael Cohen (Nuance cofounder), James Giangola and Jennifer Balogh, the word "persona" is defined more specifically to the speech-recognition industry:

A more satisfying technical definition of persona is the standardized mental image of a personality or character that users infer from the application's voice and languages choices.

Computers with Personality

But why should a speech recognition system or computer have a personality? In *The Media Equation*, Byron Reeves and Clifford Nass concluded that "Computers, in the way that they communicate, instruct, and take turns interacting, are close enough to human that they encourage social responses."

Their experiments were patterned after those conducted by psychologists who study politeness in human-to-human interaction. In one experiment, participants viewed facts presented in text on a computer screen. The computer later gave the people a test and identified which answers were right and which were wrong. The computer then informed the participants how it (the computer) had performed. It said it had done a great job.

The participants were divided into two groups to evaluate the computer's performance. Half were assigned to answer the evaluation questions on the same computer that had just praised itself. The other half answered the identical questions on a different computer located on the other side of the room. What happened? The participants who answered questions on the same computer gave significantly more positive responses than did participants who answered on a different computer.

We found the exact same differences with voices as we did in the earlier studies that used only text. When a voice on a computer asks about itself, people are more positive and less honest than when they are asked questions by a different voice on a different computer or when they give their responses on a questionnaire. The conclusion: Users are polite to computers whether they use text or voices.

THE MEDIA EQUATION
By Byron Reeves & Clifford Nass

It's the same when someone asks, "How did I do?" on a particular effort. Praise is served up in large doses. If their effort was not very good, most of us would want to be polite and not hurt their feelings. So, if we are indeed attributing human characteristics to computers, it makes sense to ensure that the computer's personality is one that customers can be comfortable with on a regular basis.

It's like going to the bank, lunch counter or store where the staff is always cheerful and greets you with a warm smile and welcome. It feels good to be appreciated. We know a speech-recognition system is not a person, but if we are going to respond to it as if it were human, shouldn't we invest the time and resources to make it as pleasant an interaction as possible?

This gets down to business and money very quickly. Who do you like to spend your money with? Someone who's bored and doesn't pay much attention to you? Or someone who's consistent, pleasant and effective? It's a no-brainer. If it's true in real life with real humans, why would it be any different when attributing human characteristics to technology?

The Brand-Persona Connection

Creating a persona for your organization is a collaborative team effort. Once the business needs and high-level objectives are identified, the team is assembled. In the early years, these projects were often relegated to the technical staff. Today, however, C-level executives are getting involved sooner because the impact on the organization is so large.

At the very start, the players who "own" the brand need to be involved. Their duty is to ensure that the brand message is on point day in and day out in all areas of the business.

The rest of the team includes interface designers, scriptwriters, voice coach, audio engineers, and ultimately, the voice actor.

The first order of business is typically a brainstorming session where the team members attempt to fence in the definition of the persona. Like any creative session, this is full of ideas and ramblings.

Persona Brainstorming Session Questions
- What is the brand?
- What does it stand for?
- Who are the customers?
- What do they want?
- What do they think of the brand?
- What are their demographics?
- Why do they buy from us today?
- Who do they expect to talk to today when they call?
- What are their pain points?
- Who would they like to speak to?
- Who are our competitors?
- What's their voice brand?
- Why would a customer buy from a competitor?

These sessions are kind of like sausage. You don't necessarily like the process, but you like what comes out! Once you get some consensus on answers to questions like these, you're getting closer to identifying what sort of persona your application needs. The best way to refine its identity is to craft a biography.

This is where it goes a little Hollywood. There are speech-recognition designers in the marketplace who really want to be directing movies in LA. Identifying a persona becomes akin to producing a feature film. While it's true we aren't making *Gone with the Wind* when creating a persona for a speech-recognition application, we are doing many of the things they do when making a movie.

In creating a movie, there are lots of people (writers, directors, producers, assistants, managers, lawyers) managing lots of activities (casting, actors, locations, cameras, lighting, contracts). You won't have that many working on your speech-recognition application and its persona, but there is much to learn from Hollywood. Just like movies, crafting a persona is part art and part science.

Who is this person who'll be answering the phone? They are very, very important and deserve your attention, because they will be answering hundreds, thousands, even millions of calls for the organization every day. The information gathered in the persona brainstorming session with will help you answer these questions:

- Is it a man or woman?
- How old?
- Do they sound mature or young?
- Where do they live?
- Are they married?
- Do they have children?
- What are they interested in?
- What's their attitude?
- Do they always have a big smile?
- Are they cheerful and professional?

As you can see, the fuzzy picture we started with is clearing up and it's beginning to take shape. There is typically a lot of debate among the team members on these questions, and there's usually no right or wrong answer. It's part of the process, part of the art. I've seen many executives and accounting types roll their eyes at these discussions, and sometimes it's warranted. It is, after all, storytelling. Going a little overboard on this important subject is still a good investment. This persona is the one representative of your company who will talk to every customer as they come to your operation over the telephone. It's a very powerful position.

Look at the truckloads of money these same companies spend on other budget items such as trade shows, advertising and public relations, and the persona has a higher ratio of client contact. An easy-to-use application with a pleasant and natural persona will not only reduce costs by automating more transactions, it will enhance customer service and retain more customers. If you err in overspending on something, this is a good place to do it.

Sample Personas

Once you start answering these questions, you're ready to create a biography of who will be answering the phone. Here are four biographies we created for the Microsoft Speech Server. As an inaugural partner in the Microsoft Speech program, GM Voices worked closely with the development team to create four off-the-shelf personas.

Laura Brooks

Laura grew up in St. Helena, California, where the major industry is wine production. Although raised in a farming community, Laura received the best education. After high school, she graduated Suma Cum Laude from San Jose State University with a Business Communications degree and met her husband Tony.

Now 29, Laura is a newly married customer service manager for a national retail chain. Because of her inexhaustible enthusiasm and attentiveness to customer needs, she was promoted to this position after only three years with the company. Being from northern California, she has no discernable accent. Although very articulate, her soft, clear voice reflects her desire to provide assistance to everyone she comes in contact with.

Laura loves her job and the day-to-day customer interactions. But she also values her weekends, because she gets to spend time with Tony and their German shepherd, Vino. Both outdoorsy, Laura and Tony also love hiking in the mountains and sailing. They also enjoy fine restaurants and good wine.

Kim Evans

Raised in a small midwestern town, Kim is the older of two daughters. She remains very close with her family, even though they are no longer within driving distance. She always thought she would stay in her hometown and raise her own family there.

But after high school, Kim decided to break out on her own. She went away to attend the University of Rhode Island to study marketing. School was important, but so was the social aspect of college. Holding the office of student body president and being on the swim team took up a lot of her time. Dates were never hard to come by, but Kim's friends always took priority.

On a girls' night out to Newport, Kim met her now-husband of 11 years, Bill. As a Naval officer, he had to travel quite a bit during their first couple of years of marriage. This gave Kim a chance to travel the world—something she probably wouldn't have been able to do without Bill. Visiting foreign ports of call and being exposed to new and exciting cultures helped Kim develop her appreciation for all people and her willingness to make them happy.

After Bill's retirement from the Navy, they settled in Ohio with their two children (7 and 5 years). As vice president of marketing for a small bank, Kim handles customer questions and requests regarding new products and offers. Her smooth, round voice puts customers at ease and makes them feel she is looking out for their best interests. When she is talking to a caller, she images them as someone from her hometown. Each caller is to be handled differently and each has his or her own special needs.

Greg Sheffield

Greg is the youngest of five children. He was born and raised in Houston. His large family and community passion for football instilled in Greg a strong sense of teamwork and commitment to helping others.

Greg attended Texas A&M on a full football scholarship. He loved playing the game, but his studies were even more important. He took a teacher's aid position with the history department, which helped him become a better student while helping his classmates. Completing his doctorate in psychology with honors, Greg was a hot commodity on the job market. He was recruited by a number of Fortune 100 firms as their customer/employee liaison and vice president of HR.

Skilled in the art of human interaction, Greg has played the role of customer service rep, friend, confidant and employer. His voice inflects—no bored monotone here—as it mirrors understanding of the customer's concerns. He repeats what the customer says in other words that show he truly understands the problem, has his arms around it, and can resolve it.

Greg has been married to Gayle for a little over 11 years. They live in an upper-class suburb of Houston with their three children—Judy, 9; Sammy 7; and Tim, 5. They also have three golden retrievers. There is no free time with three kids in sports, but when they do get away, they like camping and fishing.

Sam Watson

Growing up in Boston provided Sam exposure to many diverse ways of life. His hard-working parents instilled a strong work ethic in him: Focus on what you want and you'll most certainly succeed. They put him through four years at Boston College, where he was surrounded by many well-to-do friends. He worked weekends while they got to play. Sam knew it would all pay off.

Sam, who just turned 32, took a job with a manufacturing firm and quickly rose to the position of lead product designer. He is in constant contact with customers: getting feedback and suggestions and sometimes fielding support questions. Sam is determined to do whatever it takes to succeed. He puts that determination to work for the customer too, because he equates the customer's success with his own.

Sam is still looking for that "perfect" woman to complete his life. He dates regularly but also likes to hang out with friends. He's an avid softball player and enjoys the sense of competition and dedication the game brings out in him.

These personas are embedded in the Microsoft Speech Voice Prompt Engine with thousands of prerecorded voice prompts. As usual, Microsoft is focused on lowering the cost of computing philosophy in the speech-recognition market. You can hear samples of these personas at <u>www.gmvoices.com/microsoft</u> <u>/expanded/default.asp</u>

Voice Prompts

Quality in Voice-Prompt Production

Quality is an overused word in business today. It seems like every salesperson in the world is screaming at the top of his lungs about how his product or her service has the very best quality. In reality, quality means different things to different people.

Quality is a broad brush you can use to paint any business-to-business relationship. "They've got great quality" is the result of a symphony of activities that culminate in the delivery of a good service and/or product. It's a painless and even easy transaction. Backstage players in production, engineering, finance, research and other disciplines make a huge contribution to the quality that is often experienced. So quality is the cumulative result of all those people whose combined experience, resources and actions provide a quality solution.

These quality rules transcend specific markets and industries and apply to most business relationships, because quality is ultimately determined by the customer and/or the customer's customer.

Since recording voices for telecom applications is both an art and a science, some aspects of quality are clearly quantifiable and others are more subjective. For purposes of this discussion, we are going to define quality in an automated voice system's persona as "naturalness." If the technology does its job with high recognition accuracy and execution, a natural and pleasant persona will make the user's experience efficient and positive, blossoming into a long-term and profitable relationship.

Why Do Prerecorded Voices Sound Mechanical?

If making the persona sound natural in a speech-recognition or touchtone application is the key, why do so many automated voice systems sound like robots? You've heard their staccato, herky-jerky voices reading account numbers back for confirmation or the awkward announcement of your bank balance. It's as if the creators wanted them to sound like machines. Why is that?

The next sections are development-level issues that you may find of interest. They'll help you understand how we got to the current level of quality in prerecorded voices in telecommunications.

Let's go back to be early days of automated voice systems like voice mail and IVR. In the early 1980s, voice mail started making its appearance in businesses across the country. Initially, only large enterprises could afford voice mail because the systems were expensive. One of the major expenses in these systems were the hard drives that held the operating software, the voice messages left by callers and the prerecorded voice prompts ("Thank you for calling," "Leave your messages at the tone," etc.).

To get an idea of just how expensive they were, look at this 2002 chart from the National Science Board. It shows how the cost of hard disk storage space has declined from 1988 to 2002. The cost per gigabyte today is about one dollar!

Cost per gigabyte of stored information: 1988-2002

Dollars (log scale)

NOTE: 2001 and 2002 data are projected.
Source: National Science Board, Science and Engineering Indicators, 2002

One of the major challenges issued to engineers was to reduce the amount of hard disk space required on the system. They attacked on several fronts:

Compression

They compressed or "squeezed" the audio files (messages left by callers and guiding voice prompts) so they'd take up less space. The system also detected the natural silence that occurs when people speak and edited it out.

Frequency Limits

Humans can only hear a certain range. Have you ever heard a dog whistle? As a kid, I thought it was a gag and didn't really make any sound. In reality, it emits a sound that is above the level humans can hear, just like a flying bat's radar. Most of us can hear sounds that are low like a bass drum (around 20 kHz) or a bell (20,000 kHz).

The most recognizable components of the human voice are found in the 350 to 3500 Hz range, which is what most telecommunication networks transmit.

Digitization Rates

When a voice talent is recorded in a studio like those at GM Voices, the analog voice is converted to a digital sound file on a computer workstation. The files are usually recorded on a PC in a .wav format or in an AIFF format on a Macintosh. Most of our voiceover sessions are recorded in .wav at 48 mHz, which is slightly better than audio CD quality. These high-quality audio files can be downsampled to any number of final telephony formats depending on the technology, brand of equipment or application. The sound qualities can vary greatly here.

You've probably heard systems that sound grainy or hissy. This is often the result of downsampling the audio files to a very low quality, which takes up less hard disk space. Think in terms of resolution on a printer. You can get 300 dots per inch (dpi) on your office printer or you can take it to a service bureau and get a 2500-dpi printout on a high-end Linotronic system.

Multiple Use

This is the main culprit in making systems sound robotic. Most systems in use today employ this process. When disk space was at such a premium, engineers realized they could reuse many of the prerecorded voice prompts on the system and thereby reduce the amount of hard disk space required to house the voice prompt vocabulary (see definition in next section).

If they recorded the number "four" once, they could play that sound file whenever a four was needed:

*You have **four** messages in your mailbox.*
*Received at **four** sixteen PM today.*
*Your account balance is **four**-thousand three hundred dollars.*
*Check number **four**-two-sixty-four cleared on June 3rd.*
*You entered seven two **four** nine, is that correct?*
*Press or say **four** for the service department.*

In the world of programming, the more efficient the code, the better. So this was a great idea when disk space was so expensive. When a programmer figures out how to save a few lines of code with a more elegant method, it's the equivalent of scoring a touchdown for the jock. After making his announcement, he should prance around the cubicles as his coworkers cheer him on and do high fives.

Unfortunately, this method continued at the foundational programming level for much longer than it should have. As the price of drives began to plummet, there were too many other priorities to address. The system wasn't broken, so it was difficult for many established companies in the marketplace to champion internal resources on this issue. As a result, there are still a number of legacy systems in the marketplace that reuse voice prompts too much, at the expense of sounding natural.

Today the competitive landscape is forcing all automated-voice-technology providers to raise the level of quality or naturalness in their systems. New companies that are not burdened by the challenges of legacy systems can program their systems to take advantage of many of the more natural sounding recording techniques that GM Voices has pioneered.

The impact of voice brands is being recognized by more corporations in the US. The natural sound quality of the persona will impact this vital link with the customer.

How Voice Prompts Are Produced

While you can dissect any process to death, we've identified three basic levels of quality in the specialized world of producing voice prompts in the recording studio. These parameters are generally addressed at the development level, but they'll help you understand in more detail why the computer telephony systems in the marketplace sound like they do today.

Quality	Description	Most Applications
1) Highest	In-Context/Persona Recording	Speech Recognition
2) Mid-Level	Knowledge of Context	Touchtone
3) Lowest	List Recording	Touchtone

1) In-Context/Persona Recording (Highest Quality)

To make the application sound as natural as possible, the voice actor must perform his/her part of the dialogue as the system will "re-create" it through concatenation (bundling a number of voice prompts and/or phrases into a complete sentence or thought). The voice coach and voice actor must understand how the prompts are concatenated into phrases and sentences. With this information, the voice coach can direct the talent to the ideal intonation and inflection.

The voice actor reads the entire sentence, then the segments are edited and digitized to various file names. When the application reconstructs the prompts into full sentences or phrases, the flow is much more natural because the sentence is being constructed and played in the same natural order in which it was recorded. Periodically, the recording engineer, voice coach and voice actor cut and paste prompts into complete sentences to ensure the concatenation is smooth and natural. This process also helps ensure that the voice talent delivers a consistent persona throughout the recording process, which may take several days. In-context recording requires more time in recording (with voice actor), editing and prosody testing.

The dialogue designer participates in the recording session in the studio or remotely via telephone patch. This remote dial-in access allows the designer or any other party to participate in, monitor and speak to all parties in the recording session. Because the designers have intimate knowledge of how the application works, they can be valuable during the recording sessions.

This is the only way to make speech-recognition personas sound truly natural. And because applications evolve and change over time, it is critical that the production facility maintain readily available reference files for future recording sessions. These files are played for the voice actor and voice coach to ensure that subsequent recording session voice files are consistent with the previously recorded persona from a technical and performance standpoint.

Preproduction Planning

This is the most critical part of the process. It is essential that the voice production team be involved early in the project. Historically, the prerecorded voice prompts for an application were an afterthought. The intricacies of the voiceover production process were not well understood by many of the developers and engineers creating computer telephony applications. I believe it's true in most professional disciplines—it looks simple and easy from the outside. But if you want to do high-quality, consistent work, the process requires a more sophisticated project management approach.

A focus on preproduction will eliminate many potholes along the way to recording a few voice prompts, creating and managing a high-quality persona for a speech application, or beginning a full enterprise-wide voice-branding initiative. Here are a few of the questions we ask in our preproduction planning meetings:

- What are the delivery timelines?
- Where will it be used?
- Who's calling?
- Why are they calling?
- Is there a voice actor selection process?
- Will there be regular updates?
- Will there be other languages?
- What technology?
- What applications?
- Which technology providers?
- How is the script being created?

Our Preproduction Guidelines sheet goes into much greater detail on every aspect of the process. You can get a copy of it at the GM Voices website: www.gm voices.com/studio_preproductionplanning.asp.

Performance-Ready Script

Many automated phone systems in the past were thrown together very quickly. The last thing the team thought about was the prerecorded voice files on the system. The focus for many years was simply on the technical issues associated with getting the new release out. This is another area where speech recognition has forced a much-needed change.

A performance-ready script must be created that presents complete sentences and/or phrases that the computer telephony system will create based on database input. The voice actor will perform the script in the persona that has been created. To expect a team to create a believable and consistent persona without this is like asking a filmmaker to create a compelling movie with the script sentences out of order.

As you'll see in the section on List Prompt Recordings, having the voice actor read hundreds or thousands of voice prompts without regard to how they are concatenated into sentences and phrases can't be natural. There's no way you can consistently do it that way. Sure, you may get a few phrases that sound OK, but that does not make a successful application.

Here are a few samples of what a performance-ready script looks like. Note that they are full sentences:

- *Delta Flight (2236) is scheduled to depart from (Dallas/Ft. Worth) at (7): (15) (PM).*
- *Sending (three) copies of (medical ID cards) (for your entire family).*
- *The outstanding balance as of (April) (7th) is (thirteen) (thousand) (five) (hundred) (fifty) (nine) (dollars) and (thirty) (nine) cents.*

This is the gold standard in voice prompt recording methodology. If you want it to sound natural, you've got to go through these steps. In the recording sessions, many variations on scripts are read with different inflections by the voice actor. These multiple "takes" are used in prosody testing to identify the ideal audio file to use.

For example, numbers have different sounds when they end with a hard consonant such as "eight" than when they end in a soft vowel sound such as "three." Engineers have to experiment and test a number of performance deliveries to find the audio file with the ideal sound for the majority of sequences where it will be used.

After testing and tuning, the application creates full sentences with a very natural sound.

2) Knowledge-of-Context Recording (Mid-Level Quality)

In this case, the voice coach, engineer and voice actor understand the context in which the prompt is concatenated into sentences and phrases. The voice actor can estimate rising, falling and neutral intonations noted throughout the script. This information is often communicated via ellipses that indicate whether a prompt will appear at the beginning, middle or end of a sentence.

The level of quality, or naturalness, on these systems will vary greatly depending on the skill of the production team. The majority of systems in the marketplace today were recorded using this method. It can provide a level of quality normally associated with touchtone systems, but falls far short of the persona-grade expected in speech recognition and/or broader voice-branding initiatives.

Sample Script

Windows File Name	Text to Read	Context
introqtyyh.wav	*You have . . .*	You have (3) new messages.
		You have (3) faxes.
		You have (3) dollars and . . .
inqty3.wav	*3*	You have (3) new messages.

3) Touchtone List Recording (Lowest Quality)

In this third and lowest level of quality, the voice talent is handed a list of voice prompts to be recorded without any indication of how the prompts flow and concatenate. The concatenation of phrases and sentences will undoubtedly be mechanical and robotic. There is no dependable way to make the script below sound natural. This is a typical script provided by an IVR developer.

The talent must read the prompts without any knowledge as to how they will be concatenated into complete sentences.

Sample Script

Flights	Cities	Hours	Minutes
326	Akron, OH	1	01
327	Albany, NY	2	02
328	Albuquerque, NM	3	03
329	Allentown, PA	4	04
320	Amarillo, TX	5	05
321	Anchorage, AL	6	06
323	Appleton, WI	7	07
324	Asheville, NC	8	08
325	Atlanta, GA	9	09
326	Augusta, GA	10	10
327	Austin, TX	11	11
328	Baltimore, MD	12	12

Any speech-recognition application or viable voice-branding initiative should employ the in-context or persona-grade voice prompt production process.

GM Voices Natural Numbering System

Our production team at GM Voices is led by Robert Feldman. Over the past several years, he's taken the in-context recording process to an entirely new level.

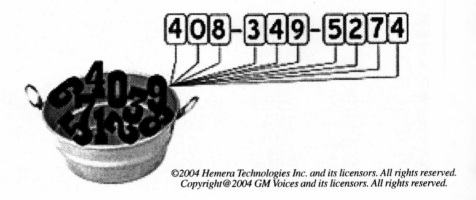

Using it as the foundation, his team has created the most natural-sounding number concatenation in the marketplace. These are foundation-level production techniques for computer telephony applications. To benefit from these advances, your platform partner must support the GM Voices Natural Numbering System. We've worked with many of the industry's technology leaders in developing this system.

First, let's look at how most of the systems today work. Number sets are usually the most mechanical-sounding part of an application. Whether it's an account number, telephone number, order number or social security number, this illustration makes it easy to see why so many systems sound like a robot.

While you are reading this, say this phone number out loud. If you're in a crowded spot, just act like you're talking into your cell phone. No kidding…do it. It's the most practical way to see why most systems in the land sound bad. The number is 408-349-5274. Now look at the bucket above. There's only one "four" in the bucket. But if you listen closely when you say the number out loud, your inflection on each "four" is different due to the rhythm of your speech. While it is difficult to hear when you say it, it screams "unnatural sound" when you hear it in a concatenated sentence.

Now look at the way a voice actor records numbers in the studio using the in-context recording process. When a three-digit string of numbers is recorded with our system, the voice actor reads this entire number in the established persona as if they were talking to a friend. The first number "four" has a bit of a rising inflection. The "Oh" sort of hangs in the air, and the "eight" finishes like a real person would. Say 408.

The main idea is say it like a real person would. In the case of four-digit strings, most people say them in sets of two. In this case, it's "two-six" and "one-nine." The first two digits need rising inflection and the last two need falling inflection. The pacing on this is almost musical. If you play a guitar or the piano, you can actually

4 0 8 - 3 4 9 - 5 2 7 4

First		Middle		Last	
1F	One	1M	One	1L	One
2F	Two	2M	Two	2L	Two
3F	Three	3M	Three	3L	Three
4F	Four	4M	Four	4L	Four
5F	Five	5M	Five	5L	Five
6F	Six	6M	Six	6L	Six
7F	Seven	7M	Seven	7L	Seven
8F	Eight	8M	Eight	8L	Eight
9F	Nine	9M	Nine	9L	Nine
OF	Zero	OM	Zero	OL	Zero

keep time with the pacing of four-digit numbers. Numbers like "five thousand" or "twenty-five hundred" are spoken differently, but those are easy programming fixes.

As you can see from this process, you will have to record more prompts, which is easy to do because you aren't reusing them like the programmers from the early 80s scrounging for extra disk space. Hard drives are so cheap today that it doesn't matter. And, more importantly, you'll end up with a much better application. Ask your technology provider if their platform supports the GM Voices Natural Numbering System.

Vocabularies

A vocabulary is the collection of prerecorded voice prompts (from a few dozen to thousands) needed for an application to communicate to the caller. These voice instructions guide the users to their desired destination by providing them the information or transaction they need.

Once the application is conceptualized, designed and scripted, it's time to think about producing the prerecorded voice prompts. While the method for generating the script will vary depending on a number of factors, such as the application, the technology provider and the company's internal process, the results need to be the same. The script needs to identify all the voice prompts to be recorded.

We've received scripts in just about any format you can imagine. It's not hard to understand why, however, because there's never been an industry-wide method for creating scripts. They might be in a Microsoft Word, Excel or Visio document. Some technology providers have even internally developed software that manages this process. They may be easy to understand or they might be a mess. The type of script needed will be dictated by the level of quality you're seeking on the final application.

There are four types of voice prompt vocabularies:

1) Base
2) Expanded
3) Application
4) Custom

Base Prompt Vocabularies

A base voice prompt is one of the core messages on the platform. It includes the basic numbers, dates, times, navigation and error prompts. Here's a sample of the script:

Cardinals	Ordinals	Months	Days	Menus
0 (oh)	First	January	Monday	...Press...
0 (zero)	Second	February	Tuesday	...activate...
1	Third	March	Wednesday	...pound...
2	Fourth	April	Thursday	...Hello...
3	Fifth	May	Friday	...for...

Navigation

If this is correct...
To transfer to another extension...
To delete all messages...
To save this message...
Press...

Error

I'm sorry, I didn't understand that, please try again.
I'm sorry, we can't connect your call at this time.
Excuse me, but I didn't get that. Can you say that again?

Expanded Vocabularies

GM Voices created the expanded vocabularies to make in-context recording/persona-grade voice prompts available in an off-the-shelf format. With over 4,000 voice prompts in each vocabulary, developers can now program their applications to sound natural at a very low cost. What would normally cost $30,000 to produce can be purchased for $99. These vocabularies focus on numbers, currencies, dates and times. Remember, they do require more disk space, but that is not an issue in today's market.

Here's a sample of the performance-ready script used to produce these expanded vocabularies:

Financial
Your service fee is 10 dollars and 91 cents.
Your current balance is 100 dollars and 37 cents.
You will be billed 215 dollars and 95 cents.
Your principal balance is 1,500 dollars and 50 cents.

Dates & Times
September twenty-first at 8:32 PM.
October fifteenth at 3:33 PM.
Friday, April seventh 2004 at 2:00 AM Mountain time.
Tuesday, January thirty-first at 9:12 AM.

Phone Numbers

407	*980*	*19-27*
407	*655*	*39-22*
713	*349*	*18-30*
212	*887*	*58-98*

Application Vocabularies

Application vocabularies are usually focused on a particular market or area of business. For instance, a specific market concentration might be providing IVR systems to small community banks. Or it could be an application targeted toward human resources departments. The number and content of the voice prompts will vary by provider because each will have employed unique procedures and techniques. These applications are very specific.

Count	Filename	Prompt *(all text contained within this column will be recorded!)*
1	T3-2007	You have reached the voice mail system . . .
2	T3-2008	For the previous menu...
3	T3-2009	Update failed.
4	T3-2010	Remove failed.
5	T3-2011	Insert failed.

Custom Vocabularies

Custom vocabularies are even more focused on the company that will use the application. If WidgetCo in Lubbock buys a speech application that allows its customers to place orders over the phone, a number of voice prompts specific to WidgetCo will be required.

- *Thank you for calling WidgetCo. We're here to help you. Just say the person or department you'd like to reach and I'll connect you right now.*
- *Great. Now, just say the catalog number for the next item.*
- *Remember, you can always have orders over $400 express-shipped the next business day.*

Voice Actor Solution Providers

You have a number of choices available in the market when it comes time to choose a voice solution. Like everything in life, there are pluses and minuses to each. Your particular situation may cause your organization to lean toward one more than the other. I'll describe the basic options and list the pros and cons of each one.

Branding is a very broad discipline that dips into hundreds of areas for an enterprise. From the little goodies given away at trade shows to the national television advertising campaign, it touches everything about the company. Speech recognition, while exciting and bringing many changes to corporate communications, is a very small part of the voice brand for most companies. This overview looks at choosing a voice-solutions provider that is equipped to address this larger view.

The voice brand is in action any time a prerecorded voice is heard by a customer. That means all these TouchPoints, are building on and adding to the brand in the mind of the customer:

Customer TouchPoints

Automated Voice Applications	*Other Voice Applications*
Automated Attendant	CD ROM Multimedia
Automatic Call Distributors (ACD)	Email
Interactive Voice Response (IVR)	Flash
Kiosks	Embedded Devices
On-Hold-Message Programs	PowerPoint
Outbound Phone Messages	Radio
Speech Recognition	Talking Cards
Text to Speech	Television
Voice Mail	
Website	

The Departments	*The Locations*
Sales	Corporate Office
Customer Service	Regional Offices
Operations	Local Offices
AP/AR	Service Centers
Finance	Call Centers
Human Resources	Distribution Centers
	Internet
	Trade Shows

Imagine creating pie charts for this mix of technologies, locations and departments. You can associate a percentage of contact with each channel or method. For many companies, the automated calls represent an ever-increasing percentage of customer TouchPoints.

We talked about in-house voice solutions in the Section "Who's Answering the Phone." Now let's look at OutSourced Voice options in more detail.

Technology Providers

This solution is usually better than the in-house option. The technology provider may include the persona and voice production services as part of their solution. There's a relatively big swing in levels of quality here.

The major technology providers have Professional Services groups that provide voice solutions. Each company professes to be better than the others, but that's only natural, right? The real story is that their internal teams oversee the entire speech application and persona creation process, which includes voice talent, production and voice coaching. The quality of their solutions is usually acceptable.

Platform Providers

These companies partner with the speech technology providers to sell their voice recognition technology solutions. The IVR providers, for example, are adding speech recognition capability to touchtone applications. Most new system sales include speech recognition. Some of these companies have their own production facilities, with varying levels of quality. Some, such as InterVoice, Edify and Gold Systems, partner with GM Voices to provide voices on some of their speech applications.

Here are a few things to keep in mind when choosing the speech technology or platform provider as your voice solution provider:

Are they enterprise-wide voice branding friendly?

These companies do a great job of getting your new speech application up and running, but are they interested in helping you put that same voice on your Aspect ACD in San Diego, the Active Voice voicemail in El Paso or the Siemens PBX in Chicago? And do they have the technical know-how to do it across any mix of technology?

Is one-stop shopping important?

While speech recognition solutions are still relatively complex, the procedures are becoming more predictable with some off-the-shelf applications that can be up and running quickly. Some customers prefer to have the speech technology provider manage and be responsible for the entire VUI, which includes the voice solution.

What are the costs?

Professional Service groups are profit centers, which means you're going to pay a lot for voice talent, production, coaching and editing services, driving up the costs substantially. They've got to add their margins.

Is the voice solution a core competency or support?

Is voice production and ongoing management a core competency? Or is it a secondary support vehicle for the main product line, such as selling licenses or turn-key solutions? Does the company own its production facilities? Does it have ongoing agreements with its voice talent?

How deep is their selection of voice talent?

The voice choices tend to be limited to small groups. Are the voices for your application the same voices on your competitor's system? How many voice talent choices do you have? How deep is their voice talent pool?

What's their turnaround and cost for small orders in the future?

These applications evolve and change over time. What is their process for providing updates for five or ten voice prompts? What's the turnaround time? Some companies order large amounts of subsequent voice prompts. What are the costs for small orders?

Independent Voice Talent

Some organizations already have a relationship with a voice talent and feel that he or she can be the voice of their brand. Or perhaps they've decided to seek out a voice independently. A Google search reveals over two million references for "voice talent." As we mentioned earlier, the voice is the tip of the iceberg. If you're going this route, there are dozens of other issues you'll have to discover and make decisions on.

Here are a few things to keep in mind when choosing to work with an independent voice talent:

What is their track record?

> Established voice talent will have a resume that details their career and completed projects. Due to the unique nature of recording in segments that are later concatenated, a good litmus test is familiarity with speech recognition.

Does the voice talent have their own studio?

> While it's not required that a voice talent have their own studio, it becomes important after the initial implementation when you need smaller updates. If your applications will be changing regularly, it's even more important.

Are they experienced in producing for computer telephony?

> Most recording studios are adept at recording audio, but when it comes time to make concatenated voice files sound natural or get them installed on telecom technology with hundreds of variations, very few are up to the task.

Will they be working with an experienced voice coach?

> Even the best actors are directed by an experienced leader behind the camera. A voice coach provides the unbiased direction required for the best performances.

Are they an efficient performer?

> Can they read the scripts in only a few takes? While this may seem unimportant, it becomes essential to keeping a consistent sound through multiple recording sessions.

Who provides the technical expertise?

> A voice talent is not going to understand the complexities of all the different telecom technology used in most organizations. They can read the script fine, but then it's up to you to get the scripts installed and running in the enterprise. If not, you—the client—may end up overseeing it.

VoiceBranding Specialists

Like any other business decision, you need to understand the options available. My objective in this section is to detail those choices enough that you can make intelligent, thoughtful decisions. GM Voices is a leading voice branding specialist in the industry, so this section will certainly expound on the virtues of partnering with a company like ours.

As voice-branding evangelists, we believe it is truly our duty to help you see the importance of selecting a provider that is totally focused on voice branding. There are just too many things to learn about the technology, the players and the implementation procedures. If you believe in best-of-breed solutions, this is clearly a unique market where they offer compelling value. Sure, companies will choose one of the options mentioned earlier for various reasons. I accept and understand this. My objective here is to make sure you have all the information you need to make the best decision.

I don't mean this to sound self-serving, but I can only accurately describe the voice branding specialist capabilities of GM Voices. Many of these might apply to other providers as well. Questions to ask:

What is their specialization?

> A company that specializes in a tightly focused area of business does it better than companies that treat it as a sideline. Not only do they do it better, but it's usually less expensive and more robust.

Do they have more voice choices?

> We have dozens of voice actors who record in our studios regularly— a wide variety of male, female, young and mature voices.

Do they record in the studio often?

> We created the Weekly Sessions program to make getting new voice prompts easy and predictable. Our voices usually record

on the same day each week. Just email a script one day and get ready to use speech files the day after they're recorded. Of course, you can get the voice any other day of the week, but using the Weekly Sessions schedule provides the best value.

Monday	Tuesday	Wednesday	Thursday	Friday
			Recording	
		Email script	Talents record	Emailed
			your script	to you

Will the sound be consistent?

Many systems you hear today have awkward changes in volume and vocal quality. We created a reference process that ensures the messages recorded today will sound consistent with the ones we recorded last year.

Do they have experience working with a broad selection of technology, brands and consulting firms?

We are technology agnostic, meaning we work across any mix of technology.

Any Technology	Any Brand	Any Partner
ACD	Aspect	EDS
Auto Attendant	Avaya	Accenture
GPS Navigation	Edify	Deloitte
IVR	InterVoice	PwC
Message-On-Hold	Lucent	IBM Global Services
Outbound Messaging	Nortel	
Public Announcements	Nuance	
Speech Recognition	Rockwell	
Website	Siemens	
Email	SpeechWorks	

Do they have experience working directly with technology providers?

We have active partnerships or working relationships with the major technology providers and integrators. Familiarity with the technology, the organizations and their people provide for smooth implementations.

Will they guarantee availability of voice actors?

> If a voice actor becomes unavailable for an extended period of time, we'll reproduce the voice prompts with another voice actor.

Do they provide translations and languages?

> Are they familiar with languages' different number sets? Can they answer gender, singular/plural conflict challenges?

PART III: STORYTELLING

The act of telling stories to communicate your message for entertainment or to drive a transaction uses skills and techniques refined over thousands of years. The characters, the plot, the tension, the solution all fall into place depending largely on the experience of the storyteller. The storyteller can be talking to you one on one, speaking to ten people at a party, or talking to millions on the radio, television or CD.

The storyteller, however, doesn't have to talk. He can spin his yarn in the text of a book, where you get to participate in the story, by creating mental images of the people, setting and time. She can tell her story with the strokes of a paint brush on canvas. Or several people can join together and tell a story in song. Storytelling is a part of just about everything we do in life.

In a real sense, your automated voice technology is one of your most important storytellers. Your automated attendant, IVR, website, on-hold messages and other voice solutions are telling stories every day. What sort of stories are they telling your prospects, partners and customers?

We're all storytellers. Most of us just don't know it, or we forgot it when we became adults. The stories we've heard, the stories we've lived through and the unfolding stories we're starring in today are an intrinsic part of who we are. The friends you enjoy spending time with and the speakers you like to listen to in person or via electronic media are good stewards of the art of storytelling. Whether they worked at it by studying some of the great storytellers or it was something that came naturally after hearing Granddad's stories for so many years, it is a very valuable skill.

Sometimes we use technology a little too quickly to communicate. It can be so fast, we forget to insert the craft into the story. It's important for us all to remember when we pick up the phone, press the send button, or talk across the table that we're telling a story. If it's our story, it's important, right? If it's important, shouldn't we take a moment to think about it? Can't we draw on the last thousand years of storytelling and make our story more compelling? Don't we want the recipient to be moved to action?

Of course, it's impossible to approach every communication throughout the day with this sort of deliberation. But shouldn't we do it on the important stories? The note to a friend, a message to your spouse or a phone call to a business acquaintance? Let's tell them a story!

What about your company? Doesn't it have a story to tell? Are you drawing on the wealth of knowledge that's been handed down for generations in the form of traditional storytelling? Let's visit the land of the story for a few minutes and see how we might be more successful when we remember that once upon a time ...

What is a Story?

A story is the sharing of experience through characters, dialogue and imagination to pass on the collective wisdom, beliefs and values of those who came before us. Through stories we explain how things are, why they are, and our role and purpose. Stories are the building blocks of knowledge, the foundation of memory and learning. They connect us with our humanness and link the past, present and future by teaching us to anticipate the possible consequences of our actions.

Types of Stories

We're all familiar with the bedtime story, cover story, fish story, life story, war story, short story, love story, ghost story, detective story, inside story, story behind the story, big story, and cock-and-bull story. What is that last one about? I've heard it for years. Turns out it's a good story in itself.

Cock-and-Bull Stories

A Cock-and bull story is one meant to deceive and/or amuse. The French variation is *coq-a-l'ane* (cock to donkey), and the Scottish version is *cockalayne.* The first known use of the phrase in America was in John Day's 1608 play, *Law-Trickes* or *Who Would Have Thought It:* "What a tale of a cock and a bull he told my father." But the term was evidently proverbial before that.

There are competing theories about the origins of "cock and bull." One source claims it's a corruption of "a concocted and bully story," with "bully" being a further corruption of the Danish *bullen,* which means "exaggerated."

Nonsense, say other sources. *The Phrase Finder* suggests the phrase came about when coaches would carry travelers to one of two inns that were close to each other on the old London Road at Stony Stratford near Buckinghamshire, England. Rivalries arose between the groups of travelers who favored one inn over the other and boastful tales were exchanged. The names of the two inns? The Cock and The Bull, of course.

The Word Detective passes along a similar story involving just one inn, the Cock and Bull, but finds it doubtful. The more likely explanation, *Word Detective* ventures, is that the expression refers to old fables featuring talking animals, a notion that the French "cock to donkey" tends to corroborate. We've seen similar usages arise in our own time, leading me to think *Word Detective* has it right and that alternative theories are not just cock-and-bull stories but—dare I say it?—Mickey Mouse.

Click on www.straightdope.com for more information.

There's also *Toy Story, West Side Story* and "Paul Harvey with the rest of the story. Good day!"

Stories by Fibbing Children

There's also the story that I, like many other kids, created to convince my mom that I didn't break the lamp. "Uhh, I…I think the window was open and the wind blew it over," I replied when she discovered it in the living room. I hadn't really made a statement. It was more of a Hail Mary long-shot pass with four seconds to go in an attempt to save myself. It sort of stumbled out of my mouth sounding like a question. With my wide eyes darting around the room for a possible excuse, I saw the window and thought of the "wind through the window" defense.

"Marc, I see your lip twitching. Are you telling a story?" she asked while raising one eyebrow and tilting her head toward me with a little smile. I immediately collapsed and came clean on the evil deed. "I was chasing Lindsay," I whimpered, glancing over to the sofa where my little sister sat quietly, trying to keep a low profile like she had no idea what was going on.

Stories by Professional Storytellers

One of my favorite stories is the one I heard at the National Storytelling Festival in the early 90s. Judith Black (www.stories alive.com) told the emotional story of Rosie the Riveter. Rosie was the character who represented all the gutsy American women during WWII who "manned" the factories as their boyfriends and husbands went off to war. Judith took the audience from laughter to tears and back again as she told this great story from American history.

To hear the best traditional storytellers in the US, you need to go to this annual October event in Jonesboro, Tennessee. There's an entire subculture of professional storytellers (www.storyteller.net/events/all) coming to a town near you. Their stories will help you tell yours with more power. Here's how the National Storytelling Association describes storytelling on its website:

---

www.storytellingcenter.net

Storytelling is as old as humankind, yet as new as this morning's news headlines. We have told stories since the beginning of time. They are the narratives of life, spanning the centuries and connecting the generations. They are the vessels in which we carry our history and traditions, our values and lessons for living, our hopes and dreams.

Storytelling encompasses virtually every facet of human endeavor. This ancient tradition is at the heart of the human experience and is just as vital today, just as much a thread of our social fabric, as ever before.

As millions of storylovers all over the world already know, there is no substitute for the power, simplicity and basic truth of the well-told story.

The site also explains how the group got started. A story by Jerry Clower on the Grand Ole Opry radio show over 30 years ago was the flash point. The story was about characters on a wild Mississippi coon hunt. High school journalism teacher Jimmy Neil Smith heard the story on that show and got the idea for a storytelling festival in northeast Tennessee.

Most of the stories these professionals tell begin in their day-to-day conversations. They add a little imagination and come up with a great story.

In the world of sales, the great storyteller likely has a competitive advantage when he or she can creatively chronicle the experience of another customer who benefited from purchasing the product or service.

"Nothing happens until something is sold," say the old-school sales-training people. I believe nothing is sold until somebody tells a good story. From a commerce standpoint, sales conversations are much the same as they were hundreds of years ago:

Yes, I want it and I'll pay you for it.
I want it in a different color. Can I get it in red?
If I buy it, will you deliver before Friday?

At the core, these conversations, these dialogues, are stories. We tell our side of the story, they tell their side. We want something, they want something, and the person with the most compelling story usually wins. In the best win-win situation, both parties get what they want.

Technology is dramatically changing the way we're telling stories. We're using the telephone, websites, email, instant messaging, television, radio and a whole host of other devices. These tools are allowing us to increase the size of our audience and extend our voices to the entire world. Even with these new-fangled message delivery tools, the keys to good storytelling will greatly determine the success of your efforts.

Storytelling Keys:
- Is it interesting?
- Does hold our attention?
- Does it entertain us?
- Is it personal?
- Will the product or service solve our problems?
- Will it make our pain go away?
- Will it make our lives better?

As Zig Ziglar would ask, "Do we believe their stack of benefits is higher than our stack of money?"

Narrative Stories

Narrative is a more journalistic way to tell a story. Not in the hard news sense, but more like the stories you read in the *Lifestyles* section of the paper. If you took a journalism class in college, you may recall the "inverted pyramid" that positions all the important information at the top of the story. The first sentence answers these questions:

- Who?
- What?
- When?
- Where?
- Why?
- How?

When I first heard this in Journalism 101 at Georgia State University in Atlanta where I attended college, I couldn't wait to get my hands on that morning's paper to see if it was really true. After class, I grabbed a paper and, sure enough, I picked out the answers to all six questions on several news stories. The concept stuck in the

Velcro of my mind and I've used it as an organizational approach to problem solving and project management ever since. From a storytelling standpoint, however, the inverted pyramid is too efficient, too cold. It's like Joe Friday always said in *Dragnet*, "Just the facts, Ma'am."

The narrative approach is found in the *Lifestyles* section of the paper where everything is more leisurely. It tells a story in a way that moves and motivates the audience. It reaches out to them and connects on some emotional level. It describes the environment, the setting, the characters and the emotions they're experiencing in a way that humanizes the story and makes you want to learn more. Connecting with the audience is key in any storyline.

Here's how *Merriam-Webster* defines narrative:

Narrative (*known*)

Etymology: Middle French, from feminine of *narratif*, adjective

1) *Scots law*: the part of a document containing the recitals; *specifically*: the part of a deed immediately following the name and designation of the grantor reciting the inducement for making it

2) something that is narrated (as the account of a series of events): *story, narration*

3) the art or study of *narrating*

4) the representation in painting of an event or story or an example of such a representation <the *narrative* of St. Francis of Assisi>

Chip Scanlan, a writer at www.poynter.org, wrote a series of articles in 2003 that dig into the art of narrative. In "What is Narrative, Anyway?" he asked reporters, writers, editors, authors and teachers how they defined it. A few of the answers appear below:

I think of narrative as storytelling: that is, as a way of ordering events and thoughts in a coherent sequence that makes them interesting to listen to. It therefore has a strong oral heritage. The sequence doesn't have to be strictly chronological, though it can be; it can include digressions and flashbacks and foreshadowings, just as a story recounted around a campfire can. But because narrative is powered by events, its goal is not essentially analytical or critical, though, like many stories (especially in traditional genres — folktales, fairy tales, fables), it can contain substantial moral lessons.

—Anne Fadiman, Author
The Spirit Catches You and You Fall Down

What we are doing is telling stories. The strict definition of "narrative" is seldom used as Fitzgerald used it in the The Great Gatsby. *Fitzgerald had a character tell us a story from his point of view. We tend to write in the third person from the omniscient point of view, thus storytelling.*

A story told using:

- *Character. In which a personality is revealed or changed.*
- *Scenes. A place described where an action occurs.*
- *Time. Used to define the limits of the story and around which action is organized.*
- *Technique. The use of descriptive writing and dialogue.*
- *Purpose. A theme or development which is of interest or importance to the intended reader.*

Skillfully done, the story unfolds, allowing the reader to meet the characters as they encounter problems with which they deal in a place and time the reader experiences with them.

— Joel Rawson, Executive Editor
The Providence Journal

Story. A narrative moves forward by dramatic and chronological sequence.

It may just move forward all the time or may move back and forth, but the reader assumes that it has a starting point (conflict) and an ending point (resolution).

Between the starting and ending point there is dramatic action. Characters act (and dialogue is action) and react. The action and reaction changes them in a way that is significant to them and to the reader.

Narrative does not (usually) tell the reader about the story as traditional journalists do, but as novelists and screenwriters do. The narrative writer reveals the story so the reader watches and comes to the reader's own conclusions about the significance of the events the reader has observed.

Show, don't tell. Mark Twain: Don't say the old lady screamed — bring her on and let her scream.

— Donald M. Murray

In business, as in life in general, there are a number of different settings and circumstances in which we find the need to communi words you use, your tone of voice and your body languinterest. This fragmentation is essentially the result of keeping their eyes on the viewers or listeners as they are divided into smaller and more focused groups. Technology has made our increased choices economically viable for suppliers.

The study of the audience is critical to any storytelling and branding efforts.

Radio

Radio station audiences are substantial for many formats:

• Rock	• Easy listening
• Country	• Heavy metal
• Jazz	• Gospel
• Talk	• News
• Christian	• Sports

Magazines

There are thousands of magazines that cover just about any interest you can imagine. From *Quilting Magazine* and *Horse Illustrated* to *All About Beer* and *Paintball Magazine*, there's an audience out there for just about anything.

Cable Television

Back in the late 70s and early 80s, when I sold cable television door to door, I never gave The Weather Channel a chance. I never paid any attention to the weather forecast, I just went about my business. "Who could possibly be interested in a weather channel 24 hours a day?" I wondered.

Maybe I was a little too self-sufficient at the time. Today, with three kids, The Weather Channel is one of the first things we look at in the mornings.

Have cable television options gotten ridiculous or what? Remember the Bruce Springsteen song with the line "57 channels and there's still nothing on"? That was back when. Now here we are in the middle of the first decade of the third millennium and there are 200 channels on cable and satellite. And talk about specialization to an audience! How about these channels:

• Animal	• Entertainment	• News
• Aviation	• Food	• Outdoor
• Biography	• Movies	• PPV events
• Cartoons	• Movie videos	• Remodeling
• Comedy	• Mystery	• Sports
• Educational	• National Geographic	• Weather

And the Internet is really ratcheting up the specialization. Creating a cable channel is relatively cheap compared to a broadcast network, because the resources required are vastly different. Using the Internet, you can specialize much more for much less. Your crazy uncle who's always coming up with wacky ideas now has a distribution channel for his Basswax Mounted Fish Polish. Throw up a website with a little search engine optimization and all those guys with a "fading" bass on their living room walls can place their orders!

Direct Mail

I get mail every few weeks from a man who says he specializes in selling homes in my subdivision. The flyer has the name of the subdivision screaming across the top of the page. There are 200 houses in my neighborhood. Wow, I guess he's the guy I'll need to call when it's time to sell my pad, no?

I also got a letter the other day from an important politician. The letter looked like it was handwritten to me. Inside was a personal note and a picture of him and his wife. Neat, we're like best buddies. All because I donated $50 to his campaign last time around.

Email

The segmentation in email is getting better. Of course, the economics of sending out millions of messages at no cost allows the spamalators, or whatever you call the people who crank out all that junk, to not concern themselves much with targeting. I can hear them now in a brainstorming session: "We're not going to waste any time on targeting. We'll just send the message to everybody."

As a side note, I was thinking about branding and the word "spam." Do you remember that mysterious canned meat? Does anybody really know what's in that stuff? When we were kids, we ate Spam from time to time. I wonder what all the talk about email spam has done for the brand awareness of Spam, that Hormel meat product?

By the way, Hormel has a funny website: www.spam.com. You can sign up for the Spam Fan Club, go to the Spam Museum, get info on the Spammobile, and even register to win a trip to Pigeon Forge. You can buy Spam hats, shirts and even underwear. I was a little surprised that I couldn't find any reference to email spam on the site. Seems like they could harness that awareness and do something with it. Or at least try to get some sort of royalty.

Where did the word "spam" come from? Here's what www.askoxford.com has to say:

---

spam

• **noun 1):** trademark: a canned meat product made mainly from ham **2:)** irrelevant or inappropriate messages sent on the Internet to a large number of users

• **verb (spammed, spamming)** send the same email message indiscriminately to large numbers of users

Derivatives: **spammer** (noun)

Origin: apparently from the first two and last two letters of spiced ham; the Internet sense apparently derives from a sketch by the British "Monty Python" comedy group, set in a café in which every item on the menu includes Spam.

Now, back to how audiences play into voice branding. We know we need to examine the audiences we're dealing with in our business. While the following categories, subsets and importance will vary due to the nature of your business, let's look at the five core audiences that most businesses should target.

Audiences

Customers

For most companies, this is the most important group. If you don't take care of them and make them feel good about doing business with you, they'll go to your competitor, who is regularly trying to steal them away. Current customers are already purchasing from you, so you must be doing many of the right things for them.

Every time customers call, your brand is being built. What is the call like for them? Most executives can't answer that question because they will not take the time to call in like a customer (see TouchPoints, page 2).

A great deal of business growth is attributed to current customers buying more. You just need to make it easier every time they buy. Needless to say, you've got to constantly be improving your operation in today's competitive environment to keep your customers happy and buying from you.

Prospects

Business growth also comes from new customers. The ratios vary depending on the type of market you're serving and the business model. The voice brand needs to give the prospective customer compelling reasons to purchase from you. Do you have an After-Hours Info Center?

Interview your current customers via telephone and record it—with their knowledge of course. Your customers are your greatest sales representatives, so put them to work for you. You can use these powerful testimonial sound bites in your voice brand by putting them in your After-Hours Info Center, on your website, and in your sales team's multimedia presentations. It's easy and costs you almost nothing!

Employees

Your voice branding effort is not targeted directly to employees, but they can be a vital part of it. They talk to customers every day. What are you saying to them about your voice brand? You can include them in your voice branding efforts. We've helped many customers use creative voice messages and talking email promotions to communicate the voice branding efforts to their staff.

The voice messaging systems most companies use are actually a broadcasting network. Email is fine for sending out policies, order information and other data-driven communication. Voice, however, is emotional, and can move employees in ways that text email never will. With a voice message from the CEO and a couple of customer testimonial sound bites, you can touch the front-line employees in a way that is personal and connects. It's not complicated; it just requires a little effort. If this is of interest, send an email to voicebranding@gmvoices.com and request our white paper "Using Voice Mail to Build Your Team."

Partners

If you're not partnering with other companies today, you're probably in trouble. It's a key tenet in business to team up with organizations that offer complementary solutions in this age of specialization. Part of your ongoing communications effort is to keep those key partners selling your solutions or bringing in deals. A crisp, clean voice brand tells everyone, partners included, that you run a sharp and efficient operation. And that's who people want to do business with.

Languages

In our global economy, the audiences are getting larger! Thanks to communications technology and transportation, the world truly is getting smaller, yet the unique nature of language and culture presents challenges. North American companies that wish to expand their markets to other countries must learn to speak and correspond in the local language for success. If you're communicating with an ethnic community in the US, you've got to speak their language combined with various amounts of English.

Over the years, we've built an extensive network of partners around the world that allows us to help our clients speak in any language. We've translated and recorded projects in over 50 languages from around the world. These capabilities fall into two segments:

1. In US Translation and Production

If the project will be used for an ethnic community in the US, the translation and voice production is best handled in this country.

2. In Country Translation, Voices and Production

Many North American based companies are selling products and services around the world. The first step in any international language project is understanding where the audio program will be heard. Who is the audience, where do they live, what is their social status? If the audience is in South Korea, for example, you need to translate and produce it there for "local market credibility."

Translation Challenges

Translation is a very specialized skill. It becomes even more complex when dealing with concatenated speech files. When adjusting a computer telephony application for other languages, it can become very complex. The English order of subject/verb/object changes in other languages. This means the programming that concatenates the speech files must change as well.

These are development-level issues, but you should know that projects get more complex in other languages.

Number Sets

Spanish: There are two versions of the number 1 (masculine and feminine).

French: There are two versions of the number 1 (masculine and feminine).

German: There are five different ways to say the number 1, and compound numbers are "backward" from English (85 = 5 and 80).

Japanese: There are up to nine entirely different number sets, and the word "three" for "3 messages" is different from that used for "3 hours" and "3 dollars."

There are over 20 world languages with more than three number sets, and any programming that is not adapted to properly handle these sets will be seriously impaired, have substandard playback, and lose market credibility. Improper use of numbers has major repercussions, ranging from appearing ridiculous to being disrespectful.

The following matrix shows how the numbers 1 through 6 vary dramatically in Japanese. In essence, there are over six versions of the number 1 in Japanese. The number "names" change as a result of use. Dates, days, digits, voice messages/faxes, hours and minutes are counted using different Japanese words.

Number	Dates	Days	Digits	Message/Fax	Hours	Minutes
1	tsuitachi	ichinichi	ichi	ikken	ichiji	ippun
2	futsuka	futsuka	ichini	niken	niji	nifun
3	mikka	mikka	san	sanken	sanji	sanpu
4	yokka	yokka	yon	yonken	yoji	yofun
5	itsuka	itsuka	go	goken	goji	gofun
6	muika	muika	roku	roken	rokuji	roppu

Address Gender, Singular/Plural, Ordinals

Spanish has two genders for nouns—masculine and feminine. A "message" is a masculine noun, while an "hour" is feminine. A change in gender requires a change in adjective. There are different words for "available" and "received" according to gender of the noun modified. Just when the programmer has adapted for Spanish, along comes German, with three genders. But reprogramming for three genders is not enough. Many Russian and Slavic languages have up to six different genders.

Changes in grammar do not end with gender. The nouns themselves may appear in more varieties than singular and plural. In English, one prompt for "message" and one for "messages" is satisfactory. It also passes for Latin-based languages. However, Russian has at least three variations: "message," "messages," and "messagi." There will also be variations in word endings according to the part of speech the word plays in the sentence: subject, direct object, object of a preposition.

Ordinals also present unique challenges. Ordinals refer to "first, second, third, etc." English-speaking creators are very fond of these adjectives, using them indiscriminately for "February 3rd" as well as for "third message." Use of ordinals in international languages is problematic. In the date "February 3rd," using the word for the ordinal "third" makes absolutely no sense whatsoever in dozens of languages. In numerous others, there are multiple variations on the ordinal words, depending on the gender of the noun modified and the grammatical position in the sentence. German and its relative languages have four different ways to say "third."

Translation Funnies

There are many stories of US companies that used poorly translated presentations and advertising in other parts of the world that were offensive to the local audience.

Here's a compilation of some of the more notable translation mistakes over the years:

1) Coors translated its slogan "Turn it loose" into Spanish, where it was read as "Suffer from diarrhea."

2) Clairol introduced the Mist Stick, a curling iron, into Germany, only to find out that "mist" is slang for manure. Not too many people had use for a manure stick.

3) Scandinavian vacuum manufacturer Electrolux used the following in an American campaign: "Nothing sucks like an Electrolux."

4) In Chinese, the Kentucky Fried Chicken slogan "Finger-lickin' good" came out as "Eat your fingers off."

5) The American slogan for Salem cigarettes, "Salem: Feeling Free," was translated in the Japanese market as "When smoking Salem, you will feel so refreshed that your mind seems to be free and empty."

6) When Gerber started selling baby food in Africa, they used the same packaging as in the US, with the beautiful Caucasian baby on the label. Later they learned that, in Africa, companies routinely put pictures on the label of what's inside, since most people can't read English.

7) Colgate introduced a toothpaste in France called Cue, the name of a notorious porno magazine.

8) An American t-shirt maker in Miami printed shirts for the Spanish market that promoted the Pope's visit. Instead of "I saw the Pope" (*el Papa*), the shirts read "I saw the potato" (*la papa*).

9) In Italy, a campaign for Schweppes Tonic Water translated the name into "Schweppes Toilet Water."

10) Pepsi's "Come alive with the Pepsi Generation" translated into "Pepsi brings your ancestors back from the grave" in Chinese.

11) We all know about GM's Chevy Nova meaning "It won't go" in Spanish markets, but did you know that Ford had a similar problem in Brazil with the Pinto?

Pinto was Brazilian slang for "tiny male genitals." Ford renamed the automobile Corcel, meaning "horse."

12) Hunt-Wesson introduced Big John products in French Canada as *Gros Jos*. Later they found out that, in slang, it means "big breasts."

13) Frank Perdue's chicken slogan, "It takes a strong man to make a tender chicken," was translated into Spanish as "It takes an aroused man to make a chicken affectionate."

14) When Parker Pen marketed a ballpoint pen in Mexico, its ads were supposed to have read, "It won't leak in your pocket and embarrass you." The company thought the word *embarazar* (to impregnate) meant to embarrass, so the ad read "It won't leak in your pocket and make you pregnant."

15) The Coca-Cola name in China was first read as "Ke-kou-ke-la," meaning "Bite the wax tadpole" or "Female horse stuffed with wax," depending on the dialect. Coke then researched 40,000 characters to find the phonetic equivalent "ko-kou-ko-le," meaning "Happiness in the mouth."

16) In Central American Spanish, the name of our Mexican restaurant Chi-Chi's means "titties."

17) Some folks from England got a huge laugh from the name of one of our small airlines: The Trump Shuttle (Donald Trump's airline). In England, "trump" translates into "fart"!

18) And finally, not even Nike is exempt. Nike has a television commercial for hiking shoes that was shot in Kenya using Samburu tribesmen. The camera closes in on one tribesman who speaks in native Maa. As he speaks, the Nike slogan "Just do it" appears on the screen. Lee Cronk, an anthropologist at the University of Cincinnati, says the Kenyan is really saying, "I don't want these. Give me big shoes." Says Nike's Elizabeth Dolan, "We thought nobody in America would know what he said."

PART IV: TECHNOLOGY AND TRENDS

Customer Self-Service

Trends come and go, but every decade or so, one takes root and revolutionizes the way we conduct business. For the 2001-2010 decade, the key trend is "customer self-service." Customers like it because it gives them control. Companies love it because it's automated and dramatically lowers costs. Customer self-service will be so big that we need to coin an acronym for it right now: CSS. You saw it here first.

What's making CSS possible? The digital convergence we've been talking about for the last few years is serving as the foundation for a fluid exchange of data across a number of devices and platforms. The most recognizable entrée to customer self-service is the Internet, followed closely by speech recognition and the kiosk. These technologies and our enthusiasm for CSS are significantly impacting our lives in the following (and many other) ways:

Gas Station: Self-Pump and Pay

In the 1960s, you'd never see someone pump their own gas. The service station attendant washed your windshield, checked the oil and pumped the gas. That'd be a shocker today. We've been pumping our own gas for nearly four decades and everyone is comfortable with it. In the last few years, they've also trained us to manage the financial part of the transaction by inserting our credit card into the slot before we fill up. We take the receipt when instructed by the LCD readout!

This get-the-customer-to-do-the-work strategy turned into a competitive advantage when it meant customers no longer had to stand in the checkout line behind people buying lottery tickets or struggle emotionally with whether it was OK to leave the kids in the car while they go inside. Most gas stations today also have an intercom so you can push the button for help. And as an added bonus, there's a little squeegee gizmo beside the pumps so you can wash your windshield. Just think how much more gas that store sells now that we're doing most of the work!

Grocery Store: Self-Checkout and Pay

Grocery stores have been using scanners for decades. For the first few years, I kept a close eye on the monitor that displays the price for the item just scanned. Somehow I just knew they were going to slip one through or make a mistake and overcharge me for an item. But I've stopped paying attention to it. A quick scan of the receipt usually reveals that the technology did its job correctly. I think most of us would rather rely on the computer to track charges than Wendy the cash register guru.

I suspect that scanners allowed stores to lower the job requirements for the people who do the scanning. How much does an employee need to know to grab the milk and slide it across the scanner? They don't even have to count your change anymore because the register tells them how much to give you. Do they save money because they don't require the same skill level as someone who can key prices? Did those people on the register get a pay cut? Did we get a discount?

Over time, the scanning process and its acknowledgment beeps became a regular and accepted feature at Kroger, Target, Wal-Mart and other stores. Then another self-service innovation made its debut next to the register: the credit card scanner, a device that looks like a phone keypad with a wire-connected pen that didn't have a ball point. "Boy, that one got by the design review team," I thought when I first saw it.

As I handed my credit card to the register person, she held up her hands as if I were attempting to rob her. "Oh, you can scan the card yourself now. Just slide it through the slot," she said. I was a little suspicious. After pausing for few seconds, I slid my card through. "The magnetic strip needs to be on this side," she said helpfully. I struggled through the process and ultimately was successful.

The next time I went to Kroger, there was a new section in the store where registers 10-14 used to be. Now there are four kiosks. I've since learned that "kiosk" is the Trojan Horse of customer self-service.

Airport: Self-Ticketing

I've been a frequent flyer for 15 years or so. In the air-travel business, your airline of choice is often a result of where you live and what hub is located there. I live in Atlanta, where we boast the largest, most crowded airport in the world. There's been an ongoing rivalry with Chicago's O'Hare over the years as to which is the busiest—meaning most landings and takeoffs, most passengers, most lost luggage. I'm not sure what the criteria for biggest and mostest is.

A new addition to customer self-service in Atlanta's airport is the ticketing kiosk. They first appeared in 2003, a half dozen or so in front of the ticket counters. I remember my first time trying one. The screen was a little hard to use. Instead of a "touch" screen, it was more like a "punch" screen; I had a tough time getting it to recognize my index finger's message.

I requested my upgrade, got my boarding pass and was instructed by the screen to proceed to the ticket counter where an agent would take my luggage. Sure enough, it worked. The helpful agent called me by name, checked my picture ID, and wrapped the destination tag on my luggage.

However, as I started to move toward the security area, the agent interrupted my departure. "Mr. Graham, you'll need to take your bags over to the scanner," she explained with a smile while motioning toward this huge machine that looked like an earth mover. So here's another case of customer self-service where I have to do all the work. I have to take my bag over to the new screening gizmos that must be here courtesy of our friends at al-Qaeda.

That was a year or so ago. Now the ticketing area is almost entirely customer self-service kiosks. Here's another twist: Some of the kiosks have no screens, only a telephone. I've not used one of those yet; I'm not sure how they work.

Another CSS tool that works well is the automated gate announcements at Delta. GM Voices provided the voice actors and personas on these applications, which are heard in many airports in the US. In the past, a gate agent had to speak into a microphone, saying the same thing over and over again.

Delta Automated Gate Announcement Script

Count	File Name	Prompt
1.	welcome.wav	Welcome to Delta …
2.	thankyou_gids.wav	We expect to begin boarding approximately 30 minutes prior to departure. Please watch the gate information screens overhead for additional flight information. As always, thank you for choosing Delta.
3.	carry_on.wav	Federal regulations allow one carry-on bag plus one small personal item such as a purse, computer bag or briefcase. To maximize storage space for all customers, please put one item under the seat in front of you. Remember, your carry-on item must fit in the Delta Size Wise unit located by the boarding door. If it does not fit, please see a Delta representative, who will check it for you.

This application turned out to be a big deal for Delta. Instead of agents saying the same old "yadda, yadda" into the microphone, they can be helping a customer. Multiply that times thousands of flights a day and we're talking about a huge savings. Another added bonus, no offense to the gate agents, is that now the customers can understand the announcements.

Restaurants: Self-Service

The dining world has moved into CSS in a big way. Once upon a time, you'd go to a restaurant, be seated, order, eat, pay the waitress (who's now called a server) and leave. While McDonald's probably gets the initial credit for CSS in fast food, the concept has infiltrated just about every other category in dining.

The buffet has been around for years, as has the deli, but they too have changed. Instead of filling your glass, someone now hands you a cup so you can pour your own drink. The upside, of course, is that you don't have to wait for the server to happen by when you need more soda, and you usually get as many refills as you want.

Now, instead of being served, you stand in line to order, get a tray for your sandwich, and shuffle over to the drink emporium for your ice, drink and condiments. Then off to your table where you enjoy your meal. When finished, you collect all your trash and dutifully put it in the large box by the door that psychologically screams "PUSH" so you'll know to what to do.

Customer Self-Service Timeline
1968: Pump my own gas?
1975: Get cash from a machine?
1988: Get my bank balance at midnight?
1999: Get info without five menu levels?
2001: Book flight using my voice
2004: More info any time, with speech?

Branding and Customer Self-Service

There's one aspect of CSS that reinforces the importance of branding in general and voice branding in particular. As customers and prospects become more relaxed and comfortable with CSS, what's to keep them from buying from your competitor who has access to the same technology? What keeps customers coming back? What keeps them referring prospects to you? It's the BRAND. It's all those things that make your brand better than brand X. And with all this CSS technology, you need a consistent voice brand throughout your enterprise, because that's where customers are going to be managing their relationship with your company. Your voice brand is on every piece of phone equipment in your organization. What does it say about your brand?

Look at the drawing of the technology in a call center on the following page. At every link, there's an automated voice guiding the customer. In many real world applications there's a different voice on each system!

To further illustrate the critical nature of what's happening with CCS and the brand, look at what Al and Laura Ries have to say about branding as it relates to the new way of selling when the customer is in control:

Today most products and services are bought, not sold. And branding greatly facilitates this process. Branding "presells" the product or service to the user. Branding is simply a more efficient way to sell things.

The selling is in the brand. In this age of multimedia, the verbal endorsement of a product, essentially its guarantee, is represented by the name brand rather than by the personal recommendation of a salesperson.

—Al and Laura Ries
The 22 Immutable Laws of Branding

More and more customers are not being "sold." They are instead choosing what to "buy." If the key trend is to transfer customer service over to the consumer, the brand becomes the main sales presentation.

Digital Convergence

Convergence has been a pretty hot word for a while. What does it really mean? It means the major communications channels in our lives—television, telephone and computer—are all coming together.

After years of promise, these technologies are converging. Today they all speak the same digital language of 1's and 0's. I've been hearing this 1's and 0's lexicon for years, but never could quite get a grasp on it. I'm not a technical person. I did not do well in math beyond the basics of addition, subtraction and division. In talking to other nontechnoids, I learned that I was far from alone. Most regular people in sales, marketing and customer service didn't really understand this binary numbering system with only an on or off, power or no power, charge or no charge, or one or zero choices.

You've probably witnessed a scene like this: A group of people at the office are

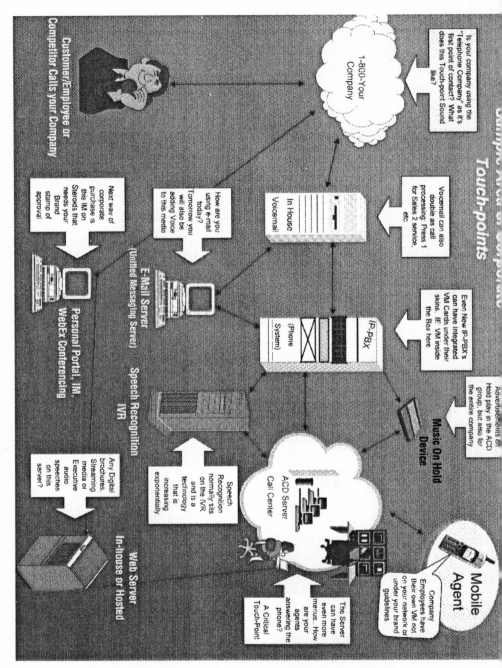

Used with permission. Mark A. Daley, Siemens Technology Consultant

pondering some equipment problem, not sure what to do. Up walks Walt, his pocket protector filled with every primary color pen and one mechanical pencil. He surveys the scene and picks up that the group is perplexed by the challenge. He leans over the equipment and then scans the crowd for a moment of unusual eye contact.

"Oh, you guys don't need to worry about that. The new one we're getting is digital," he says matter-of-factly. Everyone listening nods their head in synchronized agreement, with the accompanying "ah," as if that explains everything. Well, most of those people had no idea what Walt meant. If you were bold enough to ask, he'd drown you in a fire hose caliber dowsing of technobabble. It's a price too high to pay at that moment, so everyone goes on about their business as if they understand.

Hey, listen…I understand there is an engine under the hood of my car, but I have a 30,000-foot view of how it works. I take the car into the shop occasionally, where they tweak it up and change the oil. This is all I need to know. I think that's the same strategy most people employ for understanding digital 1's and 0's. I use a computer. I turn it on, launch applications and create documents. If it breaks, I call the help desk and someone fixes it. I think it's a great example of the specialized work force. I would be doing a disservice to the organization if I "wasted" my time trying to figure it out.

So the lines between telephone, computer and television have become blurred. It's becoming hard to tell where one stops and the other one starts.

We used to only use a phone. Now we:
- Listen to voice messages on a computer
- See who the message is from onscreen
- Forward a voice message with notes in an email
- Email a picture taken with a cell phone

We used to only use a fax machine. Now we:
- Get a fax on the computer screen
- Send a fax from the computer

We used to only use a DayTimer. Now we:
- Look at our calendar on a personal digital assistant (PDA)
- Synchronize contacts data to the cell phone each morning
- Look on the network to coordinate staff schedules

We used to only buy CDs. Now we:
- Download music from the Internet to the PC
- Transfer music to the MP3 Player

We used to only use the postal service. Now we:
- •Get the neighborhood newsletter PDF via Email
- •Go to a website instead of a catalog and 800 number
- • Receive overnight mail and packages by express courier

We used to go to the camera store. Now we:
- •Download pictures and send to family and friends via email
- •Modify, touch up and print at home (no developing fees)
- •Have a library of photos on disk and hard drive

We used to only watch broadcast or cable television. Now we:
- •Watch DVDs on the computer on the plane
- •Watch DVDs on television at home
- •Watch DVDs on a personal DVD player anywhere
- •Access Internet on TV
- •Record movies on TIVO

We used to only read email. Now we:
- •Listen to email via text to speech from phone system

In the future, it will be any device, anywhere, anytime.

Speech Recognition and User Interface

What is a "user interface" and why is it important? If you're looking for a definition in the traditional *Merriam-Webster* or *Oxford* dictionaries, you won't find it. That's generally a testament that it is a relatively new term or area of study. Interestingly, you will find the term at www.dictionary.com, which is a multisource online electronic dictionary not burdened by the rigorous methodologies required for entry in the old-school printed reference books.

User Interface *(noun)*

(computer science) a program that controls a display for the user (usually on a computer monitor) and that allows the user to interact with the system [syn: *interface*]

Source: WordNet ® 1.6, © 1997 Princeton University

So the UI is the place where humans and technology meet. The most common UI is the one associated with computers: the "graphical user interface" or GUI.

The transfer of design skills from the graphics/brochure-oriented world to the GUI is typical of how new disciplines evolve and grow in business. Remember how the writers and stage actors from Broadway adjusted their talents toward the new medium of radio in the 1920s? It's the same process.

The UI is where we control the gizmos, gadgets and machines that make our lives easier. The keyboard and mouse bring you the computer, the dashboard brings you the automobile, and the LCD/keypad takes you to much of the rest of technology. Most UIs consist of "what you see" and "what you do."

The most profound exception to what you see and what you do framework is the most ubiquitous piece of technology in the world—the telephone. The telephone added "what you hear" to the UI equation. What do you do first when making a call? You listen to confirm there's a dial tone, right? See if it's true the next time you pick up a wireline phone.

The dial tone's sound came about mainly because telecommunications equipment around the world can recognize it, says Lucent Technologies/Bell Labs spokesman Adam Grossberg. It was introduced in 1903 and became more prominent in the 1920s. Back then, it was one frequency. The one we hear today was introduced in 1963, designed not to interfere with other frequencies in the TouchTone system.

—William Weir
"The Sound of Silence: Death of Dial Tone I in the Cellular Age"
The Hartford Courant

In addition to the dial tone, more sound was added to the UI equation: busy signals, off-the-hook alarms and intercept messages explaining that "the number you dialed is not in service at this time."

Computers make awful sounds when there is some sort of error, keypads now beep when you push the buttons—we have a lot of sound coming at us.

Speech recognition, however, is different. It brings sounds to us, yes. But it's the first device that listens to what we say, understands the meaning and takes action based on what you said. The challenges are much greater because the UI in speech is time-based, not spatial like a computer screen. The system has only one chance to get it right in the interaction. You can sit there and noodle around with the options in graphically presented information.

Family of Technologies

Speech recognition actually represents a family of related technologies. Industry insiders refer to the business simply as "speech." While it has functioned as a subset of the telecommunications industry for a number of years, speech is rapidly expanding to new areas like Global Positioning Satellite (GPS) navigation, games and toys.

Scientists at a number of universities including MIT in Boston and the University of California at Berkley have been working on speech recognition for decades. For many of those years, the processing power of computers, and ultimately PCs, was not enough to meet the demanding needs of speech recognition. In the late 1980s, the capabilities of PCs began to meet the new methods being developed in speech, and commercial applications began to appear.

The technology has passed bleeding-edge status and is now helping many Fortune 1000 companies lower costs and improve customer service.

Speech recognition technologies include:

Speech Recognition
- Recognizes user responses and takes action
- Works used in dictation software such as Dragon Naturally/Speaking

Speaker Verification
- Uses digitized voice prints to verify identity

Text to Speech
- Computer speaks with sounds patterned after a voice talent

Speech Recognition Technology Timeline

Year	Event
1936:	First electronic speech synthesizer invented at Bell Labs
1941:	Touchtone phones invented
1950s:	Early work on speech recognition at Lincoln Lab using computer-based pattern-recognition techniques
1958:	System for digital conversion of speech by David, Mathews and McDonald
1960s:	Shakey the Robot developed—world's first mobile robot with ability to reason
1967:	Vertibi introduced an algorithm for finding an optimal solution that has been used extensively in speech recognition
1970s:	Work began on computer voice response, talker, verification and automatic speech recognition
1970:	The Hidden Markov Modeling (HMM) approach to speech recognition was invented by Lenny Baum

1971: DARPA established a Speech Understanding Research (SUR) program to develop computer systems that could understand continuous speech

1971: IBM achieved the first voice or speech recognition software for computers

1978: "Speak and Spell" introduced by Texas Instruments and speech chip led to huge strides in development of more human-like digital synthesis sound

1980s: IBM introduced the Tangora System, a speaker-dependent isolated speech recognition system

1989: Speech-driven robot developed

1995: Product for voice dictation of Mandarin Chinese offered by Apple Computer

1996: Charles Schwab became the first company to devote resources toward developing a speech recognition IVR system with Nuance

1996: BellSouth launched the world's first voice portal, called Val and later Info by Voice

1996: Large-vocabulary continuous-speech recognition systems capable of error rated below 5% for most speakers

1997: Dragon introduced Naturally Speaking, the first continuous speech dictation software

1998: Phone Web introduced as alternative to standard IVR systems

2000: TellMe introduced first worldwide voice portal

2000: NetBytel launched the world's first voice enabler

2000: Nuance and Speechworks went public

2001: AT&T Consumer Services launched *How may I help you?*

2001: AT&T unveiled Natural Voices System

2002: Voice pattern authentication introduced

2002: 511 traffic reports became available via cell phone in San Francisco and Utah (provided by Nuance)

2004: ScanSoft introduced OpenSpeech Attendant

2004: ScanSoft introduced SpeechPak 1.0 for Utilities

2004: Nuance packaged voice authentication of caller with Nuance Caller Authentication 1.0

2004: Microsoft launched Speech Server

Source: John Kelly, Speech Technology Magazine

Business Applications

It is primetime for speech. Much of corporate America has implemented successful speech applications in its operations or planning to do so, including:

Airlines/Travel
Continental
United
Delta

Banks and Credit Cards
Bank of America
Wachovia
Wells Fargo

Brokerage
Charles Schwab
E*Trade

Retail
Wal-Mart
Pitney Bowes
FedEx
Phillip Morris
Hanes
PayPal.com
HP

Insurance
Pacificare
United Health Care
Humana

Other
Fandango
Exxon
Paramount Pictures
Dominoes
USPS
Alcoa
MSN
AGL Resources

Return On Investment (ROI)

When the staff sends the recommendation upstairs that the company needs to buy new technology, the executive will view this proposal through his or her ROI lens. It must deliver on two key points: It must (1) lower expenses or (2) increase revenue. If it doesn't stand up to cross-examination here, don't bother writing it up.

The good news for speech recognition is that it does both dependably.

Lowering Expenses

In the call center environment, there are dozens of tasks that customer service reps handle over and over again that can be turned over to speech enabled automated systems. Remember that people love customer self-service now. If you can make it easy for customers to answer simple questions with automation, it's a better experience for them as users. Your brand goes up in value because you're making their life better! Here are a few prepackaged speech applications from several providers that will help lower costs:

<u>*Off-the-Shelf Speech Applications*</u>

Account payment	Job hotline	Prescription refill
Address change	Name/Address change	Speech-enabled
Appointment	Order status	Outlook
confirmation	Patient lab results	Stock portfolio
Automated attendant	PIN reset	Store locator
HR benefits		Telephone banking

Increasing Revenue

This is a secondary point in speech recognition. Ultimately, increasing the successful call-resolution rate and increasing customer satisfaction will lead to a more powerful brand, which leads to more revenue.

Justification	Rank
Reduce operational costs	1
Increase successful call-resolution rate	2
Increase revenue per agent interaction	3
Increase customer satisfaction	4
Increase self-service options for Callers	5

Source: Kelsey Group ROI Study, June 2002

Voice Brand Audit Presentation

Hopefully, at this stage, you see the value and importance of creating and managing your corporate voice brand. If you don't yet see it, I invite you again to hear hundreds of voice brands at www.top100voicebrands.com.

The most logical place to start with any initiative is to determine the current status. In the case of your voice brand, it only makes sense to conduct an assessment of where it is today. Don't be misled to think you don't have a voice brand. You do. It's what your customers hear today when they call. Most voice brands are a collection of mismatched voices, wildly varying volume levels and call flows that haven't been reviewed since the system was installed.

To help you understand the Voice Brand Audit process, I'll start at the end and work back to the beginning. Imagine you're in the conference room with your branding team to review the Voice Branding Audit we created for your organization. We'll pretend that your company is the WidgetCo sample we described earlier.

The team consists of the marketing coordinator, Kelsey; the marketing communications manager, Darren, and the chief marketing officer, Hunter. The meeting belongs to Darren, who hired GM Voices to create a TouchPoints Report CD ROM as the first step in an enterprise-wide voice branding initiative.

"We've gotten the TouchPoints Report and I think you'll find it interesting," announced Darren as he held up the CD jewel case with the WidgetCo logo on it. "They called over 50 of our offices just like our customers do, recorded the calls and now we've got 'em all on this CD so we can listen to them. This is when we learn what our voice brand sounds like."

"How long is this going to take?" asked Hunter as he looked at his watch. "I've got to go to lunch with Don to cover some stuff on the Zeller deal." Don is the CEO of WidgetCo and the Zeller deal is the largest order WidgetCo has ever closed. It's a $35-million-dollar project. Technically, it's a done deal, but Mr. Zeller...that's THE Mr. Zeller...wants to make a formal announcement at Zeller Manufacturing's main facility near Dayton. The deal could have gone to an offshore provider, but Mr. Zeller wants to make a bold statement that keeping business in America is good for everybody.

"It'll only take a few minutes," responded Kelsey as she nodded her head at Hunter. "I've got everything queued. Let's get started. I think you'll find it interesting as the marketing guru." She clicked the start button. "Last week we spent a few hours with Diane and Rick in Telecom going over this material so we'd have a better understanding of all the technical stuff." As she said this, the LCD projector that hovered over the conference room table threw a map of the United States up on the screen. "Here you can see all the WidgetCo locations around the country. There are 164 remote sales offices and...."

"I don't mean to be rude, but can we get to the bottom line here? I've got a lot to prepare for Don," interrupted Hunter apologetically.

"Bear with me a second; this'll be worth it," replied Kelsey as she held up her hand in a nonoffensive hang-on-a-minute way. "The ones with circles are the offices we can listen to right now," she added, sliding the mouse across the screen and clicking on the circle in Denver.

"Thank you for calling WidgetCo. Our menu has changed..." came out of the speaker. It sounded like the woman saying it was bored. She rambled on for about ten seconds before Kelsey pressed another circle. This one was over Eureka, CA. "This is WidgetCo. If you're calling during business hours, listen to this menu of choices...." The voice on this one was deep. It sounded like the guy might work in the shipping department and recorded the message in the warehouse with people talking on the phone in the background. "Is that what our customers hear when they call in?" asked Hunter as he squinched his eyes up in a "wow, that's not good" sort of face.

"Let's listen to a few more," suggested Kelsey without waiting for a response or agreement. Over the next minute and a half, she played about 15 seconds of the automated attendant greetings from Phoenix, Tulsa, Moline, Grand Rapids, Mobile and Charleston.

"That is what our customers hear every time they call," added Darren.

"Those are really bad. How long have they been like that?" Hunter asked as if it were rhetorical. "We'll spend $16 million dollars this year on advertising, trade shows and media to convince people to call in to buy and we sound like a basement operation. That definitely doesn't fly with the new specs on our branding efforts."

"It actually gets worse," Darren said. "Kelsey, play the on-hold program in Buffalo. This guy missed his calling as a carnival barker." This on-hold program featured a big-voiced dude who sounded like a caricature of a top-40 DJ.

After only a few minutes, of this, Hunter was bummed out. He, after all, is responsible for the every aspect of the brand in the marketplace. How could he have missed this? "I guess I've never called the field offices and listened. That's really not good at all," he said. He daydreamed for a few seconds about how many thousands of customer phone calls flowed through their operations every day and the image it's projecting. It made him wince again.

The CD ROM had more samples to review, but he wasn't interested in hearing more. He knew they had a problem that had to be fixed. The TouchPoints CD had several other sections that Kelsey slowly slid the mouse over.

"The good news," declared Darren as he rose up a bit in his chair, "is that we now know what we've got! This is our starting point. These are the other steps involved with a voice branding initiative." He stopped for a few seconds on each one. "This is the Action Plan, here's the section on Crafting Your Voice Brand, and this part is called Roll-Out. You'll like this Voice Branding Brainstorming Session. That's a meeting where we identify how we think the WidgetCo voice brand and personas should sound.

Voice Branding Brainstorming Sessions
1. Company Mission
2. Business Description
3. Technology
    a. Capabilities of systems dictate the quality
    b. Rolling out a brand must be planned to accommodate multiple
    types of equipment

c. Frequency of calls
- Internal application that will be called a lot should be concise
- Infrequently used applications may have more instructions for use

4. Target Market
a. Who will hear it
b. Why they are calling
- Support, bank balance, quotes
c. Mindset of target group
- An irate customer wouldn't appreciate a chirpy voice on the support line
- An older person calling about insurance may not trust a young hip-sounding voice
- Technical personnel will understand words that nontechnical people won't

5. Competition
a. Identify
b. Study their brand

"I know you've got to leave, but you really need to hear this," Kelsey added as she clicked on the 'Sample Voices' button. She played a sample of great-sounding voice actors. "All we have to do is spend a little time listening to these samples so we can pick out the WidgetCo voice actor. There's even a section on 'Your Competitors' where they rank our voice brand against our competition. They're recorded on the CD ROM, too."

"Guys, this truly is great work. So you've got a plan to fix it?" asked a visibly relieved Hunter.

"We've got all the legwork handled already. We just need to look at the cost to see where it comes out of the budget," advised Darren. "Looks like we can squeeze some funds out of advertising and some out of tradeshows to cover the investment. Here's the proposal from GM Voices. Just need to get your approval. Rollout for the entire company will take about 60 days."

Hunter stood up to leave for his meeting with Don. "You guys are awesome. This is great work. You came in with the problem and the perfect solution."

"Thanks," replied Kelsey and Darren at the same time. Darren continued, "I'll put a voice branding brainstorming session on your calendar for next Thursday. We'll spend two hours discussing the WidgetCo brand and what we think the

WidgetCo voice brand should sound like. The creative director from GM Voices will be here to facilitate the meeting."

"Super. I'll be sure to tell Don that you two are all over the voice branding thing," he added as he shook Kelsey's and Darren's hands and walked out. They looked at each other and thought "slam dunk!"

PART V:
TOP 100 VOICE BRANDS

When I first started writing this book, my intention was to somehow identify the "status" of voice branding in America. Where does corporate America stand as it relates to the quality of the voice brand? How do we identify the companies that have great voice brands? What about the companies that have horrible voice brands? After we pinpoint the companies with great voice brands that support their overall brand, how can we rank them in quality?

Documentation

We knew we could document the voice brands around the country using the techniques we've refined over the past few years in our Voice Brand Audits and TouchPoints Reports CD ROMs. We could certainly call the numbers, record what we heard and put them in a multimedia format that would make it easy for people to review. Interested parties could simply point and click to hear hundreds of actual voice brands. That part was pretty cut and dried.

Identifying Top Voice Brands

Because of our role in the industry, we are familiar with many great applications from the various trade shows and user conferences we've attended over the past couple of years. So we started with a good book of knowledge on some of the better voice brands, but we knew there were many out in the marketplace that we didn't know about. How could we identify them?

We called on all our friends in the speech recognition and branding industries to nominate voice brands they felt were among the best and should be considered for any ranking of excellence. We got a huge response from industry insiders and have hundreds of entrants that will be considered and judged.

Judging

We've assembled a world-class committee of industry experts to evaluate the nominated companies and identify the Top 100 Voice Brands in America. This website will allow professionals who see the value in voice branding to "benchmark" their company's best efforts. We believe the time is right for corporations to recognize the value and importance of their voice brands.

Funny Voices

In addition to the Top 100 Voice Brands, there is a section dedicated to documenting those that are "less than ideal." Some are downright funny. If, after calling a company, you ever thought,

> *"That phone recording is horrible."*
> *"That voice is strange. Do they know how that sounds?"*
> *"I can't understand what they're saying"*

then you can nominate that company to be considered in the "less than ideal" voice brand category.

You can nominate a company, listen to samples of those nominated and learn more at www.top100voicebrands.com

Suggested Reading

The Media Equation by Byron Reeves and Clifford Nass

How to Build a Speech Recognition Application by Bruce Balentine and David P. Morgan, Enterprise Integration Group (2001)

The Art and Business of Speech Recognition: Creating the Noble Voice by Blade Kotelly, Addison-Wesley (2003)

Voice User Interface Design by Michael H. Cohen, James P. Giangola and Jennifer Balogh, Addison-Wesley (2004)

The 22 Immutable Laws of Branding by Al Ries and Laura Ries, Hooper Business (1998)

Emotional Branding by Marc Gobé, Alloworth Press (2001)

The Design of Everyday Things by Donald A. Norman, Basic Books (1988)

The End of Marketing As We Know It by Sergio Zyman, Harper Business (1999)

Websites of Interest

www.brandchannel.com

www.brandweek.com

www.reachcc.com

www.landor.com

www.businessweek.com/pdfs/2003/0331_globalbrands.pdf

www.gmvoices.com

ABOUT GM VOICES

GM Voices, Inc., specializes in producing audio treatments for a variety of applications, including telecommunications, speech recognition, multimedia and Internet web pages. With dozens of voice actors working remotely from studios around the world via ISDN lines and world-class voiceover recording facilities in its North Atlanta studios, the company produces thousands of prerecorded voice segments weekly.

Today, the never-ending drive to lower costs through automation is being realized most effectively with speech recognition technology. Applications such as call routing and transaction processing save companies millions of dollars annually. The technology works. GM Voices makes sure it has the right personality or persona, with a stable of professional voice actors and voice talent readily available.

The voice is critical to success. GM Voices provides corporate voice personalities to companies including Dell Computer, Delta Air Lines and Cingular Wireless. As the architect of these valuable voice brands, GM Voices gives voice to technology.

Today, the company's creative, engineering and account service teams develop a variety of audio programs, personas and voice branding solutions for Fortune 5000 and communication companies. GM Voices, Inc., helps companies enhance their image and communicate with customers, suppliers and employees more effectively. www.gmvoices.com

ABOUT G. MARCUS GRAHAM

Like most successful entrepreneurs, Marcus Graham recognized an opportunity and took steps to turn the opportunity into a business. In 1983, after hours recording for Atlanta-based Rich's department store did not present a positive image to callers. Management agreed; and hired him to upgrade their phone recordings. Soon after, GM Voices opened its doors.

Since 1985 Marcus Graham, founder and CEO of GM Voices, Inc has been helping Fortune 1000 and communications companies develop and enhance their image through a variety of audio programs, personas and 'voice branding' solutions. He continues to develop innovative communications programs for a number of business applications.

Providing high quality prerecorded voices from professional actors for telecommunications applications was the company's foundation. Since that time, the telephone, computer and television have converged to create a vibrant communications environment that requires millions of pre-recorded greetings, prompts and messages.

In the ensuing years, Marcus has become an industry expert in making the overall interface easy to understand for the user and effective for the application owner. His expertise and enthusiasm for public appearances has made Marcus a sought after speaker to industry and general groups on a number of topics including communications, networking, entrepreneurship and selling.

He has also been featured in numerous trade and general business publications including *Speech Technology Magazine*, *Call Center Magazine*, the *Atlanta Business Chronicle*, the *Atlanta Journal Constitution* and *The Wall Street Journal*. His professional career includes a number of years in commercial radio (WFOX and WSB) and cable television marketing/ sales.

Marcus is a member of the Atlanta Chamber of Commerce and numerous industry groups. He's performed Stand Up and Improvisational Comedy at local clubs. He also teaches at a local high school through Junior Achievement. He enjoys golfing, hunting, reading, playing guitar and the outdoors and spending time with his family. He lives in North Atlanta with his wife Karen and their three children Rachel, Kelsey and Hunter. They attend North Point Community Church.

To have Marcus speak at your next meeting, to order more copies of *Voice Branding in America,* or to order a talking book on CD (read by Marcus), visit www.gmvoices.com, e-mail Valerie Hayden at vhayden@gmvoices.com, or call 770-752-4500.

NOTES

NOTES

NOTES

NOTES

NOTES

NOTES

NOTES

Printed in the United States
22360LVS00005BA/22